Online Tradi:

Masterclass

Complete Beginners Guide to Trading

Stocks, Forex & Cryptocurrency with

Swing, Position & Day Trading Guides +

Investing Techniques from Great Investors

Written By

Alpha Bull Traders

The following Book is reproduced below with the goal of providing information that is as accurate and reliable as possible. Regardless, purchasing this Book can be seen as consent to the fact that both the publisher and the author of this book are in no way experts on the topics discussed within and that any recommendations or suggestions that are made herein are for entertainment purposes only. Professionals should be consulted as needed prior to undertaking any of the action endorsed herein.

This declaration is deemed fair and valid by both the American Bar Association and the Committee of Publishers Association and is legally binding throughout the United States. Furthermore, the transmission, duplication or reproduction of any of the following work including specific information will be considered an illegal act irrespective of if it is done electronically or in print. This extends to creating a secondary or tertiary copy of the work or a recorded copy and is only allowed with express written consent from the Publisher. All additional right reserved.

The information in the following pages is broadly considered to be a truthful and accurate account of facts and as such any inattention, use or misuse of the information in question by the reader will render any resulting actions solely under their purview. There are no scenarios in which the publisher or the original author of this work can be in any fashion deemed liable for any hardship or damages that may befall them after undertaking information described herein.

Additionally, the information in the following pages is intended only for informational purposes and should thus be thought of as universal. As befitting its nature, it is presented without assurance regarding its prolonged validity or interim quality. Trademarks that are mentioned are done without written consent and can in no way be considered an endorsement from the trademark holder.

Financial Disclaimer:

I am not a financial advisor, this is not financial advice. This is not an investment guide nor investment advice. I am not recommending you buy any of the stocks listed here. Any form of investment or trading is liable to lose you money.

Accuracy Disclaimer:

All prices and market capitalizations are correct at the time of writing. Price and market cap information is sourced from official sources. All information in this Book was derived from official sources where possible. Official sources meaning literature that is publicly available, provided by the company or official company website.

This Book contains "forward-looking "statements as that term is defined in Section 27A of the Securities Act and Section 21E of the Securities Exchange Act of 1934, as amended by the Private Securities Litigation Reform Act of 1995. All statements, other than historical facts are forward-looking statements. Forward-looking statements concern future circumstances and results and other statements that are not historical facts and are sometimes identified by the words "may," "will," "should," "potential," "intend," "expect," "endeavour," "seek," "anticipate," "estimate," "overestimate," "underestimate," "believe," "could," "project," "predict," "continue," "target" or other similar words or expressions. Forward-looking statements are based upon current plans, estimates and expectations that are subject to risks, uncertainties and assumptions. Should one or more of these risks or uncertainties materialize, or should underlying assumptions prove incorrect, actual results may vary materially from those indicated or anticipated by such forward-looking statements. The inclusion of such statements should not be regarded as a representation that such plans, estimates or expectations will be achieved

Disclosure: At the time of writing, Alpha Bull Traders did not own shares of any of the stocks named.

Contents

Position Trading

Market Timing Mastery — Trade Like a Hedge Fund Manager by Discovering How to Spot Trends and Knowing Exactly When to Buy & Sell Your Stocks for Maximum Profit

Introduction

Gaining control over money is something that everyone in this world has pondered about at some point in their lives.

When it comes to the money that you have with you, you have a fair amount of freedom to decide on what you want to do with it. You can choose to save it. You can splurge it on getting that new car that has so many features, it might as well be the next Batmobile.

But imagine taking a large sum of money and placing it on an investment for a long time with the expectation that it will generate a profit. You cannot do anything you want with that investment. You cannot control it by nudging it towards the direction that you want it to go. It just follows the trends and eventually gives you a result after the period you have set for it. This is what position trading is all about, and despite how it sounds, more and more people are joining the ever-expanding world of trading.

Many amateurs ask, "Can someone make a living out of trading?" Since many so-called traders put their life savings on the line, the question seems pretty valid. Even if you are merely investing a small portion of your earnings, savings, or budget, it is still your money. So, there is no easy way to answer the question. Yes, you can earn big in trading; with enough successes, it might just seem like you are in the process of turning it into a career path. On the other hand, the path to success is a difficult one. In fact, it might just be one of the most difficult paths to take to make a living.

We have to constantly put ourselves in a position where we are going to face psychological discomfort and stress. And let's not forget the monetary stress that comes from knowing that your money could disappear forever, never to return to your hands again. Think of trading like the act of rowing downstream. You cannot control the river, but you can control your rowing. The world of trading is the river, and the act of rowing is you getting a control over your mind and emotions.

It may sound frightening, but the rewards are equally big. If you play your cards right, you won't have to work for an entire year while making your dreams of traveling come true.

So, what do we do in order to get good at the game of trading?

Before we find out an answer to that question, there is something that you should know: there is no secret technique or a get-rich-quick method for working on trades. The people who have gotten good at trading aren't using shortcuts, or the latest magic system they bought from some guy on the internet. They worked on their skills, learned from their mistakes, and kept evolving until they were good at what they do. They eventually developed strategies that helped them understand how to trade effectively.

So, what you need is not a secret technique but a consistent structure and a strategy that you can use to successfully understand the trading game and make informed decisions. In fact, do you want to know what sets trading pros apart from the rest? You might be rather surprised by the results. Here they are:

- Great traders are opportunists. If they notice others reacting uncontrollably, they take advantage of that fact and try to capitalize on it.

- They are always aware of the latest trends. In fact, they know about the new trading methodologies that dominate the market.

- They are well-versed in the fundamentals of trading. They understand that you need to build a solid foundation to become good at something.

- Headlines are important. But you must know how to interpret them. When you are trading, keeping a close watch on the headlines gives you an idea of what you should be doing with your trades.

- Most importantly, they don't dwell on their disappointments for long. To them, every disappointment is one way not to do things. They understand that every mistake puts them closer to the right way of trading.

- Professional traders usually have a few strategies that they employ when they trade.

Now, you might read the above statements and wonder if that is all there is to becoming a great trader. Shouldn't there be a line about how great traders are using a particular type of system that gives them access to incredible strategies for making easy money? While there are systems and strategies that can help you with your trades, there is no way to make *easy* money. By using the word "easy," I am referring to a trade that has minimal risk but gives you a big return without any challenges.

One of the things to realize when you get the opportunity to watch amateur traders is how much they do <u>not</u> embody the above statements. They are impatient to get in on a trade, they skip learning the fundamentals. It is possible for them to let their emotions get the better of them, which can lead to costly mistakes. They might completely lose track of the latest economic and political news that concern their trade and end up losing their money.

Let's try and see two scenarios.

In 2018, a financial analyst from Vancouver decided to take action on a volatile market (Malito, 2018). The 24-year-old earns $50,000 a year. He decided that perhaps it was time to strike rich. The next thing you know, he lost all his lifesavings (which was close to $100,000) on his trade.

That sounds rather grim. In fact, no one would like to be on the receiving end of that situation. For some, it might signal the end to a trading career before it's even begun. Your mind must have drifted off towards your life savings, wondering if you are going to lose all that money. Not so fast, I have another real-life scenario for you to consider.

In 2015, a trader made a big bet (Diaz, 2015). He hedged his chances on the probability that semiconductor firm Applied Materials ($AMAT) might just get to break new heights. As it turned out, he was right. He made a cool $1.74 million in two days. Of course, if his bet was wrong, then he would have lost $1.74 million!

The two stories above highlight something important: anyone can win or lose big in the trading game. The entire process does not have to be complicated. All it requires is a keen mind and a few profitable strategies. When you have the right strategies, you can set up a successful trading position, which in turn provides you with a lot of benefits.

- You deal with less stress compared to other traders in the market. Day traders usually face volatility and high risk of losing all their capital. Position traders are saved from both, though.

- When you are engaged in position trading, you are using a long-term strategy. Traders use these long-term strategies to keep their positions open for days, weeks, and sometimes even months. Other forms of trading devise plans that are focused on short-term results. This means that methods that are not focused on position trading are open to attacks from short-term risks.

- In a position trader, the traders do not remove their trades from the market, even when the market is heading in the other direction. The traders do not exit too early, unlike other forms of trading. For example, in day trading, people might end up pulling out their trades with a loss. When you are a position trader, your biggest tool is your patience as you wait for the right level to take the profit.

- Position trading has a very hands-off approach to trading, which is not the same when it comes to intraday trading where you are doing due diligence every day in order to avoid a monetary catastrophe. In a position trading, one only has to periodically monitor the trading position.

Here's an example of how one works with position trading. In 1999, the firm of trader Jim Chanos had analyzed the activities of Enron, a popular energy company. While everyone else was hopeful about the company's rise. Predicting the growth of the company, Jim Chanos had a strong belief that it was lying about their position and financial status. Trusting his belief, his firm started a short position, which was essentially a move where assets were sold in order to generate a profit from the fall or dip in the value of the asset. Jim strongly believed that Enron was going to end up in a disastrous position. Of course, he held his position for more than a year. But eventually, his predictions came true when Enron filed for bankruptcy in 2001.

Just how much profit did Jim Chanos make because of his prediction, you ask? A whopping $500 million.

All it took was for Chanos to have keen insights, the right strategy in place, and of course, the ability to stay abreast of the latest information (and to interpret them as well).

In the case of Jim Chanos, he had the advantage of years of experience. But all of those advantages, skills, insights, and understanding of the market had a beginning, a foundation.

And that is what you are going to receive.

This book will give you the foundational structures to help you navigate the complex world of position trading. It will become your guide to slowly build up your confidence and discover strategies that you can implement on your trades.

But as I have mentioned before, there is no get-rich quick scheme or secret technique to achieve that. While these tools are here to help you, they are not going to be of any use if you do not take actions to implement them. You are still going to be the one making decisions and facing the risks. You are still the one who will have to get back up from losses, should they happen.

In fact, if you think that someone is promising you an easy method to make money quickly off position trading, then you can be certain that you are probably being hustled. Every form of trading, whether position or currency, carries its own set of risks. Sure, the levels of risks are different between trading methods, but so are the rewards and the frequency at which you can get them.

Welcome to the world of position trading where the right management of money and financial strategy will allow you to achieve profits from three to 10 trades a year.

Chapter 1: What Exactly Is Position Trading?

The world of trading has gone through numerous stages of evolution. Today, based on your financial goals, you can choose a strategy that works best for you or a trading form that matches the amount of time you can devote to it. The modern investor has numerous tactics in his or her investment toolkit that complements the strategy being used.

One of the tools available to investors is what we call position trading.

In position trading, traders hold on to their stocks for an extended period of time. It may last anywhere from a few weeks to even years, which makes position trading the opposite of day trading (in which decisions are made almost every day). To a position trader, short-term influences, financial news, and price motions are of no concern. They are focused on the bigger picture and long-term market influences. On the most fundamental level, position trading relies on long-term historical patterns and general trends. Traders use them to decide what trades they would like to work on.

The Power of the Pareto Principle

Many people know what the Pareto Principle, also known as the 80/20 rule is. It is a universal law used for a lot of projects and activities, from learning languages to managing. If you haven't heard of it, that's okay.

Essentially, the 80/20 rule states that you are going to get 80% of your results from just 20% of the effort you put into your work. In all honesty, the split of 80 and 20 is an approximation, but the general idea behind the rule is the same. If you are working well, then you are using a small percentage of your efforts to generate big results.

At this point, you may be wondering, "What does this have to do with trading? Does it mean that we might be able to generate most of the results of the trade by using 20% of our efforts?"

Yes and no.

While the 80/20 rule does apply to the process of trading, we are looking at something else. In particular, the stocks.

You see, 80% of the price movement of stocks happen on 20% of the days. This is in direct opposition to the fact that trades make extreme shifts frequently, such as on a daily basis.

However, what happens during the remaining days when the price is not making extreme shifts?

It's simple, the market trends sideways. A market becomes a sideways market or experiences a sideways drift. When the latter takes place, then trades fall within a predictable range without resulting in any major or dramatic change.

But just because there are no major changes does not mean that the market has become stagnant. On the contrary, the market is still active. It just means that price shifts are not rising or falling beyond set parameters or levels. This makes the market very predictable. You know how high trade prices will rise and how low they will dip. There are no surprises. The level of ambiguity has just been lifted, even if for a temporary period. What it means is that decision making is much easier during a sideways market than other, more volatile, times in the market.

Why does this happen? What causes prices to change?

It has got everything to do with the principle of demand and supply. When more people begin to buy a particular stock than sell it, then this action increases its demand and reduces its supply, which in turn increases its prices. Conversely, if more people were selling trades rather than buying it, then that would increase the supply and lower the demand, creating a price drop.

The concept of demand and supply is one that many people are familiar with. However, the idea that traders would prefer one stock over another is a little too complex to understand. What makes a trade more demanding that others? Why does demand and supply keep on rising or falling? What is going on in the minds of the traders when they like a particular stock and dislike another? There are no easy answers for any of the questions about trader behavior. However, there is a basic understanding of the trader mindset and the relation that mindset has with stocks: the direction the price of the stock moves is an indication of how much value the traders think a company is worth. This eventually decides whether they are buying the trades or selling them.

Position Trading vs. Buy and Hold

Another term that you will come across quite often when you are trading full-time is the concept of buy and hold. Essentially, in a buy-and-hold strategy, you keep an investment for a long period, hoping that the price will rise over time. You typically pay less transaction fees and lower profit taxes, too. However, with those advantages comes the fact that you need to have a lot of patience to see the payoff from a buy-and-hold trade. But wait a minute: that sounds rather familiar. It does oddly bear resemblance to another form of trading that we have mentioned earlier: position trading. Both strategies may just seem like twins with different names.

However, what separates the two is the degree of chance that one places into the trades themselves. When you are using a buy-and-hold strategy, you are basing your decisions on the long-term prospects and improvements of the company. You are looking at what it has planned. You try and see how bright the future of the company is. Upon noticing that it can make tremendous progress, you invest in its growth. You are not concerned about the volatility of the market or the economic changes that occur frequently in the market. You are looking at the vision of the company's leaders, their growth targets, innovation strategies, and other components of the company itself.

On the other hand, position trading takes into consideration various factors other than the company itself. It focuses on trends and changes. Think about the trading style of Warren Buffet, one of the most renowned traders who focuses on position trading. He believes in two key principles while trading; one is to have patience and the other is to understand the market. When you think about it, position trading does not seem all that different from buy and hold. However, you are ignoring one of the key components in Warren Buffett's strategy: understanding the market.

Market understanding separates position trading from buy and hold. When you talk about the latter, you are placing your bets on an optimistic view of a company's future position. It is akin to having blind faith in a particular trade. In position trading, you are trying to understand the market as well.

Let's try to explain the idea with an example.

Assume that it is 2007, and you are looking at the value of Nokia. In that year, nearly half of all smartphones sold around the world were made by Nokia (Minds, 2018). iPhone barely existed back then and controlled a measly 5% of the global smartphone trade. By looking at the position of Nokia, you think about the future. You understood the company's goals and ideas. With the way things were going, there seemed to be nothing that could topple the dominance that Nokia had on the market. You feel truly optimistic about the brand's future and use a buy-and-hold strategy to predict that you are going to get a profitable return in 5 years.

Sadly, your predictions would have been disastrous. In less than 5 years, Nokia's market value had declined by 90%. If you had indeed hedged your future trades on Nokia, you would have been the owner of a losing stock.

Let us now look at what a position trader would have done. He or she would have looked at Nokia's position and see its immense growth. So far, nothing has differed from the strategy used by buy and hold. However, position traders also look at the overall market, including the performance of other brands.

For example, they do not look at iPhone's share in the market and think, "Bah! Just 5%? You cannot topple the Nokia giant, you Apple peasant! Go back and cry to your motherboard!" Rather, they might look at it and think to themselves, "Well, that's a 5% control of the market, which is a result of a rise that was a long time coming. Based on market factors, it seems like the iPhone may rise even more in the future. Plus, we are talking about Apple. They are known for their quality products. I feel like this phone — combined with the technology of Apple — might just change the game."

For position traders, the entire market is littered with valuable information. They consider all of these things so that they can arrive at the right conclusion. It is true that they cannot make the market predictable, but they are exerting the power of knowledge to make their decisions as concrete as possible. Here are a couple of statements to sum up the difference between buy-and-hold and position traders.

- Buy and Hold: Yes, I think this might happen in the future.

- Position Traders: Yes, I think this might happen in the future because of the following reasons.

Position Trading vs. Swing Trading

The term "swing trading" comes up in conversations about trading. However, the difference between swing trading and position trading is as obvious as night and day.

When you are a swing trader, you enter into positions and then exit them in time spans that extend to one or a few days. In fact, one way to understand swing trading is by thinking of it as a slower form of day trading where transactions occur on an hourly basis.

Compared to day traders, swing traders look for the highs and lows in the price of a particular trade. When they look at such patterns, they are able to make predictions about the value of the trade. However, their predictions cannot be made for the long-term. They can use their knowledge for the immediate future, occurring within the next few days. Think of swing trading is the slower version of day trading. When you think of it that way and compare it to position trading, the latter is like watching a snail move. There is going to be little progress in the present but come back later and you might find the snail (a.k.a. trade) in a different location. For those interested in Swing Trading, we have compiled a beginner's guide, which is also available on Amazon and Audible.

Retail vs. Institutional Traders

With the technology available today, getting into trades is not a complicated scenario. One can start trading with the push of a single button. Still, it does not mean that all traders are the same. There are some noticeable differences, especially when you consider the case between retail and institutional traders.

Let us examine both types of traders individually.

Institutional Traders

One of the most noticeable traits of institutional traders is that they are able to work with large trades. This is because they are typically backed up by a firm or entity that has a lot of capital to spend. Institutional traders also have access to various forms of trade that are not usually made available to retail traders, such as swaps and forwards.

Many times, institutional traders work with large volumes of shares. Because of this, they can eventually affect the share price of a security. By purchasing large volumes, they show that the demand for the security or trade has increased, thereby creating an effect on the value of the security.

Now, let us look at the other end of the spectrum and push the spotlight on retail traders.

Retail Traders

Retail traders often invest in futures, options, bonds, and stocks. Most of the time, retail traders work with lots (which are exactly 100 shares), but they can choose to work with any number at a particular time.

The trading amount that retail traders use in a transaction is small and often based on their budget. However, they do pay more transactional cost because they use brokers to make their trades.

Where institutional traders can impact the price of the security, retail traders do not have such power because of the low transactional costs that they have to incur.

The Bottom Line

Apart from the methodology used by institutional and retail traders, there is also a difference in the thought processes between the two.

Retail traders are often prone to strong reactions because of their emotions. On the other hand, institutional traders are focused on taking actions. They want to remove the emotion from the equation and work with logic and information.

Retail traders can forget to understand the importance of mastering the basics. Institutional traders, meanwhile, realize that their level of expertise is based on the fact that they need to master the basics.

Retail traders are concerned about their losses. To them, each loss is a major setback. Institutional traders can afford to make losses since they are backed by institutions that have large finances.

Now that you know about the two different types of traders, you might wonder if there are special times during the day when you can trade. There are, and we are going to learn more about them.

During Open Hours vs. Aftermarket Trading

The people who are introduced to the world of trading know that stock market trading hours are from 9:30 am to 4:00 pm, Monday to Friday. Every day, billions of trades are conducted in the American stock market alone.

However, what most new traders won't realize is that the stock market is open even after the market session has ended. This means that traders can work from 4:00 pm to 8:00 pm. This time frame is known as the aftermarket trading hours.

But is there a difference between trading during session hours and after them? Does it impact the trades in any way? It actually does.

During open hours, the markets deal with billions of transactions. Things only change when the market session closes. During the after-hours sessions, only a small percentage of the total volume of trades are being worked with. This means that traders have to think about their strategies even more in comparison to when they were trading during regular hours. The real question, however, is whether one can make money when trading in the aftermarket hours, considering they now have to work with limited trades.

The truth is that they can, but they might have to perform thorough research first. Here are some things to think about.

Company Announcements

When companies release information about themselves, such as their performance or financial earnings, they need to be strategic about it. If they release the information during market working hours, then it might cause traders to take impulsive actions — since quick decisions mean getting in on the action early — that might not take into account the true value of the stock of the company. This results in some serious repercussions. Let us take an example to explain this scenario.

Assume that the company announces their latest earnings, and they are worse than the last quarter. This can cause traders to impulsively move out of the stock so that they can minimize damages. However, it has a detrimental effect on the company. Because of the move-out, the company might suffer huge and unnecessary losses. In order to avoid such incidents, companies try to release announcements after regular working hours.

Now, check this: the value of the stock continues to move even after the market has closed because of the aftermarket hours. This means traders can access stock values that are often made public due to company announcements. They can use these values to make quick decisions about their stock. It is important because once the market reopens, the prices of the stocks have already changed, by which time those who had already taken advantage of the information received during the afterwork sessions have made the best use of it.

Now, that sounds pretty incredible. In fact, you might be thinking right now, "Why isn't everyone taking advantage of this system? Is this author telling me something that only an elite few know? Am I part of a high-society club and now has access to tons of information?"

Not exactly. You have to understand that not all companies release information after the market closes. Think of it as a gamble in which you are hoping that a company releases information for you to catch.

What's the Catch?

While you might have the advantage of information, there are some disadvantages to trading during aftermarket hours.

Among the biggest ones is that the market is much less liquid than trading during open hours. While you may have the advantage of time, you may not always have the benefit of liquidity unless it is a big move that has a major impact on a company.

Another disadvantage lies in the fact that there might not be a lot of people trading during aftermarket hours. This means that you might not be able to easily sell your stock.

Finally, if you discover that a company's earnings have dipped, and you would like to sell your stocks, then you might not be able to in certain cases, especially when you are dealing with smaller, non-blue-chip companies.

The biggest advantage to trading aftermarket hours, on the other hand, is that you are probably two or three steps ahead of everyone else in the decision-making process. Meaning, you can make a profit on news that you have been expecting for some time. Alternatively, you can decide if you would like to exit a stock if certain unexpected news gets announced. In the world of trading, being ahead in the game allows you to take effective decisions before the value of the stock goes in a particular direction.

No-Trade Zone

When talking about during trade hours and aftermarket, one might ponder if there is a situation where there is little or no trade on a particular stock.

That can happen indeed.

We refer to them as gaps, and they are sections on the chart where the price of a stock moves upwards on downwards sharply. These drastic changes have minimal or no trading in between. Why, you may ask?

For instance, we are under the assumption that a company's earnings are higher than expected. The company, in turn, chooses not to release this information during trade hours. Rather, the news comes out during the aftermarketing trading hours. At that time, only a few traders are able to take advantage of the news. The next day, when the stock market opens, the company's stock might "gap up." Meaning, the stock price showed a much higher opening as compared to the closing on the previous day. Between the previous day and the morning of the new information, there is a gap in the charts.

Trading Lifestyle

One of the important things to note in position trading is to take your lifestyle into consideration. You need to plan your trades so that they can complement your lifestyle. You should not be changing it to match the trades because then you might face psychological and emotional stress.

When you are trading, you need to be in the right frame of mind. This allows you to focus and think with clarity, absorb all the information, and prevent you from jumping to conclusions about any trend. Sure, the stock might look like it is getting better, but is it the money-making breakout that you have been waiting for? Is it the stock that is going to get you enough money that you might retire on a private island of your own with a glass of martini in your hand? Or will it affect your finances so much that you might consider renting out your room on Airbnb to get back what you lost?

Even if losses occur, you should be in a state of mind where you are minimizing the degree of loss by creating your plan Bs and Cs. By doing this, you are not leaving anything to chance. You are creating alternatives and options so that you are prepared for anything. We will go more into depth later on in this book when we cover money management, portfolio allocation and exact numbers to be aware of when trading.

Even if you have been a buy-and-hold investor, and you are deciding to shift to position trading, it is always important to match the trade to your lifestyle. You may believe that buy and hold might seem similar to position trading, but it genuinely isn't. In fact, assuming that the two trading forms are similar might be your first mistake. You cannot simply transfer the strategies you have been using in buy-and-hold trading to position trading.

Chapter 2: Best Trading Software

Sometimes, you might come across people saying that a trader is often as good as the trading software that he or she uses. That might not be entirely true since your attention to details, ability to gather information, and general sense of awareness of the market are all important factors that come into play when considering your level of expertise. However, one cannot deny the huge impact that trading softwares have on the traders.

For many modern traders, a trading software is indeed their window to the world of trades. Softwares allow the trader to see patterns and trends. It allows them to make predictions, decisions, and investments.

You simply have to browse online to see the different softwares that are available for you to use. From independent developers to brokerage firms, you are going to find a plethora of options, each option providing you with their own unique set of features and options. But then again, while browsing through all the different softwares available to you, you might notice that some softwares are meant for scanning while others are for trading.

So, what is a scanning software? Are they similar to a trading software?

Let's take a look into that.

Trading Softwares

With the growth of the internet and the connectivity it offers, there is an increase in the number of trading softwares. Additionally, with the easy availability of application development software, you now have trading software in popular application stores, such as iTunes and Google Play Store.

Trading software allow the users to trade and manage their trading accounts. They can make use of the various additional features like charts, forums, or even live economic news. All of them are provided to make trading easier for the users.

When you are looking into trading software, one of the most important decisions you will make revolves around what software is good for you. For example, some trading softwares provide automated features that might suit some types of traders. Apart from the features, you have to consider their fee structure, overall performance, analytical tools, and many other factors that match your trading style.

Scanning Software

A stock scanner or screener is a software that traders can use to filter stocks based on certain parameters. Scanning softwares come with free services (but with limited features) or with paid subscriptions (providing more advanced features). But regardless of what form of scanning software you choose, they both work with the same principle: they allow the users to find a trade based on a specific criteria or profile.

Let's take an example to show what scanners can actually do. If you are looking for a stock based on a specific price criterion, then you can input that criteria into the software and you will receive results of trades that match that criteria. This can be done with other parameters that include average volume, market capitalization, price change percentage, and various other criteria.

Some scanners also allow you to search for trades based on technical analysis data. For example, you can look at a particular data and choose if you would a stock to be above a particular level or below it. This helps you to plan out where you would like to enter your trades and how you would like to exit them as well.

Many traders often use the above method to find trades that look like they are going to perform better over a long period of time (which is essential for position trading).

By analyzing numerous stocks at the same time, traders can weed out those trades that do not match their requirements.

Best Online Brokers

Now that we know the difference between trading software and scanning software, let's see if we can narrow down the best online traders or brokers that are available right now.

TD Ameritrade

Apart from the fact that TD Ameritrade has gained a reputation and following over the years, the platform is ideal for beginners who are starting their journey on a trading platform. It provides beginners all the necessary information to make important investment decisions. This is complemented by the fact that you receive numerous educational materials that guide you through the usage of the software, understanding the market, tutorials on making trade, expert advice, and lots more.

Charles Scwab

One of the features that traders will appreciate about Charles Schwab is the fact that you can start your account with $0 investment. In other words, there is no minimum amount required to open your account. Additionally, people who trade heavily might appreciate the $4.95 trading costs, which is lower than many of the softwares in the market.

Similar to TD Ameritrade, you can find numerous educational and research materials on Charles Schwab, allowing both beginners and professionals to learn something new from the platform. Additionally, traders can discover a variety of commission-free Exchange-Traded Funds (ETFs) that might appeal to many traders. ETFs are generally cheap trading options that are available to investors if they are choosing to build a diverse portfolio of investments.

E-Trade Financial

The thing that sets E-Trade Financial form the competitors is the fact that they are not just offering one app, but two different apps to cater to a wide variety or traders. In one of the apps, you can move money using a special feature called the mobile check deposit, giving you greater access to your funds. The other app is an acquisition made by E-Trade, which allows you access to a greater number of trades (as the second app is older than the first).

Ally Invest

Just like Charles Schwab, Ally Invest is opting to attract users with the $0 minimum account balance. This allows a wide variety of people to enter into the market. Another similar option that it shares with Charles Schwab is the low commission structure of $4.95 on stocks. But rather than become your typical broker, Ally Investment provides you with other options, such as forex trading, apps to manage your portfolio, and additional features for technical investors.

Full-Service Brokers and Discount Brokers

Even when you are choosing the right broker among the options available to you, you might also want to consider whether you would like to understand the difference between a full-service and discount broker.

Here are the major differences:

Features	Full-Service Brokers	Discount Brokers
Brokerage	They usually charge commissions based on a percentage value that is dependent on the terms of each trade that you execute.	They avoid the percentage model. A flat fee is usually offered for each trade.
Services	They provide more than just the buying and selling of stocks. You can receive financial advisory features, retirement planning, and feedback on your portfolio among many other features.	You are simply given a trading platform for working with your stocks. No additional services are provided by the broker.
Fee Structure	Because of all the additional features mentioned above, you are charged a higher fee. Usually, you are charged 1-2% fee based on the assets you manage.	They usually do not have any additional charges because they don't offer the extra services that Full-Service Brokers do.

Trading Options	You get a whole lot of products such as options, commodities, forex, insurance, bonds, IPOs, and more.	You are mainly dealing with stocks and commodities.

Looking at the features of the two forms of brokers, it might be rather difficult for you to choose the right type of broker. However, you might consider using discount brokers for position trading. Here's why.

Lower Cost

Full-service brokers have higher costs and extra fees, which might not be suitable for those who are not comfortable shelling out a lot of cash on a trading platform. Another way to think about this is that the people who are planning their retirement or future goals might not want to constantly spend extra money on fees. They would use the trading platform for the purpose they want to achieve: trading. Because of the low commission's structure in discount trades, you often face low fee structures as well.

Unbiased Services

When full-service brokers offer advice, they might become biased towards a particular stock or trade. This means that they may try to sell you a particular stock more than others, not because it is necessarily good for you but because it is also in their best interests. You might not be able to catch on the sales tactics. Why would you? You did pay them to give you advice after all and for all intents and purposes — that is what they are doing. You might never think twice about what they are offering.

On the other hand, you have discount brokers. They do not provide you with advisory services. This is why they do not try to sell you a particular stock. Everything you see on their platform is a result of your own preferences and criteria.

Research and Information

While it is true that discount brokers do not provide any type of advisory features, they more than make up for it with the number of research and educational materials they provide. Typically, they cover a whole variety of topics. Because of the growing competition among various discount brokers, you might find many of them offering the latest news as well within the app. These news updates are available to you either through an updated feed or through video format (where they are connected to one of the many economic news channels around the world). This way, you might not even require an advisory service: you just have to compile all the relevant information and you have plenty of advice available for you.

Bottom Line

Choosing a discount broker works best for position trading. You are not investing too much into the platform. This gives you the freedom and peace of mind to focus on your trades. You might think that having advisory features might come in handy for you. However, this advice only tends to muddy the waters for you because you are unsure of whether you are being told to do something that benefits you or the broker.

Resources for Stock Scanning

Since we looked at some of the best brokers you can work with, it is now time to learn about a couple of scanning resources and just why you might need them.

Picture this scenario. You know what kind of watch you would like to get yourself. Perhaps it's a sports edition of a famous brand or one with the metal buckle. It could even be any type of quartz watch. Nevertheless, imagine finding yourself in a large showroom and left to your own without any guide and tasked to find what you were looking for.

That could be very well be the situation you might find yourself in if you enter trading. The only difference is that you are going to be replacing watches with stocks, trying to figure out just which stock is the best one for you to invest in a large stock market.

But imagine you had a guide who can help you navigate the complex world of stocks. All you have to do is figure out how much you would like to invest, the kind of stocks you are interested in, and voila! You have your options narrowed down and displayed right in front of you.

Doesn't that seem like a convenient way to enter into a trade? Rather than simply being inundated with information about so many trades that make feel like you are never going to start anywhere, why not have a few options to work with?

This is why you need a stock scanner. In general, almost every trading platform comes with its own version of a stock scanner. However, their version might be so rudimentary that you might not be able to get too much valuable information, or you might not be able to make accurate searches.

However, for that, you have another solution. You can make use of a stock scanner to get the right results.

So, having said that, are there any stock scanners that are recommended? Yes, there are.

ChartMill

This stock screener provides you with numerous tools that will aid you in your trading journey, which you can use to easily analyze and monitor the markets. With its innovative and detailed filtering capabilities, you will be able to conveniently filter through socks based on various criteria.

For example, you can filter your stocks based on sector and price, allowing you to focus on the kind of companies you would be invested in. You can also choose the industry, giving you greater accessibility to choose a specific type of company.

Along with the filtering options, you also get the option of using charts. The charts have a clean interface that is easy to navigate.

Additionally, if you would like to check a stock further, you can make use of the stock analyzer. This tool gives you the capability to perform fundamental and technical analysis on a particular stock, giving you further details on the stock. This makes your decision-making process easier, and you have greater power to form your trading strategies.

Finally, if you are already interested in a particular stock, then you can easily find them using the search function as the tool lists each stock with their corresponding symbol.

Finviz

Finviz is another stock screener option for you.

With the screener feature, Finviz shines more than the other brands in the market. This is because of the easy-to-use interface that makes navigation smooth, even for first-time users who are quite alien to stock screeners.

One of the unique aspects of the platform is that you can input the criteria yourself and receive every stock option possible that matches all or any of the criteria. You have even more search option tools on the platform, including options to search the prices based on market capitalization, outstanding shares, RSI, and even a specific candlestick pattern, which is a graphical pattern of showing the rise and fall of a stock. That last option is the standout feature of the platform because it allows you to use a particular strategy you have been building onto the platform and find stocks relevant to that strategy. However, the aforementioned search criteria are just some of the ones you can use. There are many more available on the platform that makes it easier for you to get the results that you want.

In short, you can have complete control over the stocks you would like to scan. You can even save your search criteria for later; in case you would like to go back to those options. When you have the ability to search for stocks based on numerous criteria and the capability to save your criteria, you are saving endless hours looking at your charts and backtracking to previous choices.

Finviz also provides you with heatmaps that show how valuable a particular stock is, as well as various charts that you can use to analyze your stocks. However, the downfall to the platform is its pricing structure. While you can use the free version, you won't be able to access all the best features and your screen is going to be littered with a whole lot of ads that is simply going to ruin the interface for you.

News Sources

Now that we focused on trading platforms and stock scanners, aren't we forgetting something? We are going to be making big financial decisions after all. Where are we going to get the information to make the right decisions?

From the news, of course.

So, does that mean you will need to be in front of your television set or laptop, looking through various channels until you find the right one?

Thankfully, that won't be the case if you have a platform that is dedicated to bringing you news about stocks, the market, and other relevant financial information.

Enter: Scoop Markets.

One of the things that makes Scoop Markets unique is that you can get all the news coverage about stocks and prices on one platform. It prevents you from mindlessly looking at multiple sources to find the information that you need.

You have a watchlist feature that allows you to add certain securities. Once done, you will start receiving information and updates about the security that you are focusing on right in your dashboard.

You can also look at any mergers and acquisitions, updates and recommendations from analysts, earnings reports, stock trades, and more. This allows you to get the right information at any time of the day.

One of the standout features of the platform is that you can even add certain topics to your feed, which gives you greater control over the news and information that you would like to receive.

They have both free and paid pricing levels. The forever free option lets you monitor up to 3 securities at a time, and is a great way to get a feel for the platform. Further paid options at $29/month and $69/month a month give you access to 25 and 75 securities respectively. Needless to say, just 1 good trade based on an alert from Scoop would return more than enough money to cover your subscription costs for the entire year. When starting out, you shouldn't need to monitor more than 25 securities, which makes the $29/month plan the ideal starting point for most regular position traders.

Chapter 3: Different Financial Instruments You Can Trade

Now that we have understood the various tools you can use to trade, let us now look at the securities that you are going to trade in. Starting off with the popular — and one that almost every trader is familiar with — stocks.

Stocks

A stock is also commonly referred to as "equity" or "share." It is a type of security that provides you with a portion of the ownership rights of the corporation that issued the stock. For example, if you bought the stocks of Samsung, then you have ownership rights based on the amount of stocks that you have in your hand. In addition, you are entitled to a proportion of the company's earnings and assets based on the value of the stock you are holding.

You will be able to get stocks predominantly in a stock exchange. However, that does not mean they cannot be sold privately as well. For the purpose of this book, we are going to be focusing on the things that are displayed on stock exchanges, considering they will also be available in the trading platform that you choose to use.

An important trait that you have to know about stocks is that transactions made on stocks should follow the rules and regulations set up by the government of the country the stock exchange is located in. This is done in order to protect investors and traders from fraudulent activities.

Now, the big question arises, "Why do companies raise stocks? The simple answer is that they require a certain amount of funds for either operating their business or for certain decisions.

What about ownership? How much ownership can one claim of a company?

Assume that there is a company by the name of ABC. This company has issued 1,000 shares in order to raise funds for a new technology that they would like to add to their operations. You decide to purchase 100 shares of the company, so you now own about 10% of the company's earnings and assets.

Does it mean that you can call yourself the owner of ABC?

When you purchase the stocks of a company, ou do get ownership rights where you are entitled to a portion of the company's earnings. However, you do not directly *own* the company. It is an important distinction that needs to be understood. The reason is that corporations and companies are treated like a person by law organizations. What this means is that corporations and companies have the freedom to own their own property, borrow money, face lawsuits if the situation does happen, and get other privileges that a typical person gets. This idea that a company is actually a "person" entails that the company is entitled to hold assets and even sell those assets whenever it wishes. In other words, anything that the company owns belongs to the company and not to the shareholders.

Understanding this distinction is important because most people come under the impression that they actually do own the company (or at least a part of it). So, before you go on Facebook and update your status as "Owner of Apple, baby!", understand that you are legally separate from the corporation and its intellectual and physical properties.

So, what happens to you if the company goes bankrupt?

Because the company is a separate entity from you, any case of bankruptcy does not affect you. You can actually still keep your shares with you. The only problem is that those shares might be worth nothing or the value might have dropped drastically after bankruptcy. This also works the other way around. When any of the shareholders become bankrupt, they cannot make use of the company's properties or assets to pay off their debts, as they are a separate entity from the company.

So, what does it mean when someone owns about 30% of the shares of the company? Does that make them powerful enough to take charge of the company? Not likely. Understand that it is wrong to say that one owns a third of the company because of the 30% shares. It is correct to say that one owns the entirety of a third of the company's shares.

Of course, by owning stocks, you do get to have the right to vote during the meetings held by the company. You are also entitled to the dividends of the company, based on the ahres you hold and when those dividends are distributed among the shareholders.

But what about those times when someone owns a major part of the company? Don't they technically own the company itself?

That is not true. This is the part where things get really tricky. What really happens is that the voting power of the person increases. Eventually, the person will be able to influence the board of directors of the company and even make a motion to replace them if he or she so chooses! This eventually changes the direction of the company, considering that having a new board of directors means that there is a whole new set of vision, objectives, and goals for the company.

For most shareholders, however, not being able to manage the company does not impact them greatly. They are comfortable owning a portion of the company's shares. It means that they receive a portion of the company's profits. The more shares you have, the more profits you receive. Essentially, profit-making is eventually the goal of these shareholders and power does not affect their decisions.

Another thing to note is the type of stocks.

Stock itself is divided into two main types. You have the common stock and then you have the preferred stock. When a shareholder owns a common stock, then he or she is entitled to receiving dividend and casting votes at company meetings. On the other hand, preferred shareholders do not have any voting rights. But they do have more priority over their dividends than those who own common stocks. In other words, when the company is paying out its dividends, it will first focus on the preferred shareholders and then move onto the common shareholders.

In this book, we are going to focus as the stocks as the security for position trading.

Exchange Traded Funds

A stock is a type of security. You can buy and sell it, but it is still considered as one type of security. On the other hand, Exchange Traded Funds (ETFs) are a collection of securities that is used for a particular index.

And what exactly is an index? Good question indeed.

An index (plural "indices") is a way to measure something. It is a hypothetical ruler or scale that can be used to indicate or measure the movement and performance of a price of practically anything. In the world of stocks and securities, it is used to measure the value of publicly traded goods. It does not focus on specific goods but rather an entire market or a segment of that market.

Let us take an example to highlight this.

One of the most popular indices in the world is the S&P 500. It collectively keeps a track of the performance and value of the top 500 companies in the United States. You cannot directly invest in an index. They are simply measuring tools to give you insights into stocks.

In order to work with index, you make use of ETFs. Essentially, an ETF holds the stocks that are part of a particular index or industry.

Going back to the previous example, we now know that you cannot buy from the index directly. However, what you have instead is an ETF named SPDR S&P 500 that has stocks of the companies of S7P 500 and keeps closed records and trackings of the S&P 500. You can purchase the ETF, allowing you to spread your stocks in numerous companies belonging to the S&P 500 index.

This is why an ETF does not hold one particular asset, such as the case of a stock. It actually holds multiple assets, which allows you to diversify your portfolio.

In fact, an ETF can hold on to more than hundreds of thousands of stocks scattered across various sectors and industries. Or it could even hold on to stocks that belong to a particular sector or industry. The eventual decision on which ETF to choose is based on the preferences of the trader and how much he or she is willing to invest.

Let us take another example to explain the point above now. If you were a trader, and you bought ETFs for the banking industry, then you would own stocks of various banks spread across the country.

Inverse ETFs

You can also make use of inverse ETFs. To understand that, let us get to know about how ETFs work. In a usual scenario, they make use of futures contracts to ensure that they achieve their returns. A futures contract is a type of contact where a trader decides to buy or sell a particular security at a specific price and time. This is done because futures securities allows traders to bet on the future outcome of a security. But they are not just predicting any outcome of a security. They are hoping the security or marker will rise in the future.

In an inverse ETF, the traders predict that the market will not rise, but will rather decline. If the market does decline — as predicted by the trader — then the value of the inverse

ETF will rise by the same percentage that the value of the market drops. So if a market drops by 20%, the value of the ETF rises by 20%.

This is an important strategy, especially when it comes to bear markets.

Now, it brings us to another question: What is a bear market? Does it mean you are investing in some fine-looking grizzlies?

Not quite.

In the world of trading, you will come across two commonly used terms: bull and bear market. Understanding them is fairly simple. A bull market means that the market is on the rise. The prices are increasing, and there is optimism among the traders. The market is given the name "bull" because the animal usually attacks by raising its head up, and "up" is where the bull market goes.

On the other hand, a bear market represents the market that is going down. In other words, share prices are dropping and traders are pessimistic about the outcome. The market is given the name "bear" because a bear usually swipes down to attack.

If you look at the fact that the bear market is a decline in the prices of securities in the market, then it provides the perfect opportunity for people to take up inverse ETFs, given that they will profit from the decline in the market.

Cryptocurrency

A cryptocurrency is another form of currency, and it works like one as well. In truth, you can use it to make purchases, buy services, and perform transactions like any other form of currency that you use in your daily life. The only difference is that it is entirely virtual. Cryptocurrency does not have a physical form and uses what is known as cryptography for its security. Because it is intangible and uses a complex security, it is difficult to counterfeit.

Most cryptocurrencies are not centralized. This means that they are not all regulated by one particular body, like a bank or financial institution.

What draws many agencies towards cryptocurrency? Is it the security features? Is it the fact that it is decentralized and not regulated by a financial authority? Could it be that one can create their own cryptocurrency provided they have the tools?

Actually, it's all of that, in addition to one more vital reason: it is organic.

What does that mean? Simply that is not issued by a particular body. In other words, it cannot be regulated by any government around the world. It is free of manipulation and interference from any governmental entity. It organically works with any organization because they can create a cryptocurrency of their own.

We are all aware of the first cryptocurrency to come out in the market and popularize the idea of cryptocurrencies: Bitcoin. However, that was just the beginning. Today, you only have to perform a cursory check online and you will discover thousands of alternate cryptocurrencies, each one with various features and functionalities. Some of the cryptocurrencies are clones; meaning, they replicate an existing cryptocurrency. The most common clones that you can find are those of the Bitcoin. Others are forks, referring to cryptocurrencies that are a variation of the original cryptocurrency.

Let us try to understand the example above. Assume that you have a cryptocurrency named Tradecoin. A clone would mean that someone out there created a cryptocurrency named Profitcoin, which is essentially the same as your coin. On the other hand, a fork would mean multiple coins created have more or less the same features as your coin but are not related to it. Let's say that Tradecoin 2 and Tradecoin 3 are variations of your coin, but they have some features removed or added so that they can appeal to a certain group of people.

Imagine going to a mobile phone showroom and looking at the latest iPhone. The attendant walks over to you and says that they have two versions of the phone: the 64GB version and the 128GB version. You are essentially looking at the same phone; you are only getting the freedom to choose between two different storage options. This concept of options is exactly what happens when a cryptocurrency has a fork.

Because of the decentralized nature of cryptocurrency, two parties can engage in a transaction without government scrutiny. However, cryptocurrency can be misused for various purposes, such as money laundering, purchasing drugs, and even tax evasion.

One of the ideas behind cryptocurrencies, apart from the high level of security, is that every transaction is recorded. A technology called blockchain uses a form of online ledger to store these transactions. Every new "block" on the ledger entry that is created has to be verified by all parties having access to the block. This means that if you are running a business with a couple of your friends using cryptocurrency, then every entry of cryptocurrency has to be approved by you and your friends.

However, if no transactions are supervised by governments, then how can anyone be certain that they are taking part in an official cryptocurrency deal? What guarantee does one have about the transaction that they are going to perform?

One of the ways this is possible is through the fact that many cryptocurrency transactions are a two-step process. This means that when you are about to make a transaction, you have to enter an authentication code. Once the code is entered, you will then have to confirm again whether you would like to go ahead with the transaction. This allows users to check and see if they are really interested and trust in the transaction before going ahead with it.

So, cryptocurrency seems like a profitable venture indeed. Surely, the disadvantages of dealing with cryptocurrencies could be minimal, right?

Not exactly.

One thing that makes it challenging to trade in cryptocurrencies is its incredibly volatile nature. In fact, it can be as volatile as 10 times the changes in prices as compared to the dollar. This means that you have the capacity to make 10 times the profit made using any other securities like stocks or bonds. But you also can make 10 times the losses.

The following factors cause the volatility of cryptocurrency.

- Geopolitical statements and events around the world affect cryptocurrency. For a regular currency, or fiat currency as they are called, it is affected by the country that owns that currency. In the case of cryptocurrency, news from anywhere in the world decides its future trends. This makes it highly unpredictable to see where the trend is going to go next.

- News stories that produce fear in the traders and investors also drive the value of cryptocurrency. Take for example the incident involving the closure of the online cryptocurrency platform Silk Road by the FBI (Greenberg, 2013) . The platform was a haven for all forms of illegal activities, including purchasing drugs, hiring hitmen, and money laundering. When people realized that the FBI would be getting involved in cryptocurrency dealings, their panic meter went into overdrive. They started abandoning their trades and distancing themselves for anything even containing the word "cryptocurrency."

With numerous factors are affecting cryptocurrency at once, it is no wonder that there is a lot of volatility to the currency. This is why the currency is never recommended for beginners because if you are not used to the cryptocurrency market, then you might end up making some huge losses. Those who trade in cryptocurrency is usually those who have been following the market for a long time.

Options

Options are basically instruments that you can use to buy or sell a particular asset. People can use options to deal with stocks, which is a type of asset.

What this means is that an option is literally what the term indicates: the option or choice to buy or sell a particular asset. When someone has options, they are not compelled to do a buy or sell transaction. It is entirely up to them to perform the transaction within a particular period of time.

You have two different kinds of options:

- The 'call' option allows you to buy your preferred asset at a particular price within a specified period of time.

- The 'put' option allows you to sell your preferred asset at a particular price within a specified period of time.

Each one can be attained by entering into a contract. The contract itself has an expiry date so the person who wishes to make use of the option must do so before the contract expires.

Let us look at the above security with the help of an example. Say that you are planning to get yourself an auto insurance (or any other type of insurance). You pay a monthly premium (or in some cases a yearly premium) for the insurance, which is valued much higher than the premium you pay for it.

Now, one year passes, but nothing has happened. It is time for you to renew your insurance. Even though you haven't used your insurance, you haven't lost much. This is because you had a peace of mind the entire year, knowing that any losses would be covered by your insurance. All you did in return was pay a nominal fee as premium. The only thing you have lost is the premium itself.

Think of the same idea for options. Rather than downright purchasing an entire set of stocks for a particular price, you take options. Just like how you don't exactly buy the entire insurance in one go, you are also not taking the entire stock in one go.

For instance, there is a stock of 100 shares available for $30 per share. That would mean that if you took 100 shares, then you will be paying $3,000 for those shares. Some people might find that a heavy investment. Instead, they purchase an options contract that is valued at $1.50 per contract. This means that 100 shares will be ($1.50x100) worth $150. So eventually, when you are trading, you will be trading based on your contract and its value.

With this, people will have the peace of mind knowing that they haven't actually invested a lot in the options, but they can still make a trade if they choose to.

Forex

Finally, we come to forex.

The term 'forex' is simply an abbreviation for foreign exchange. In other words, you are dealing with currencies instead of stocks of companies.

The currency exchange rate is what determines the movement of ofrex. You will usually find these currencies quoted in pairs. The EUR/USD is a popular example of a currency that is traded in the forex market. But you can always find other examples such as GBP/USD or EUR/JPY.

So, what exactly decides the exchange rate of these currencies? Is there a body of organization that simply decides how much value a currency has based on arbitrary values? Or is there more to it than that?

What drives the currency of a particular country or nation is that country's economic, political, and other factors. Unemployment, trade deficits, inflation, geopolitical events, and the levels of industrial production are just some of the various factors that decide the value of a currency. This is why investors are always glued to their television screens for the latest news updates in order for them to make quick decisions about the currencies that they are dealing with.

With forex trading, you are making decisions every day. The forex market is a very liquid market. Most people make short-term strategies so that they can make as much money as possible in the short run.

The forex market also contains a high level of trading risk. It is this risk that one should think about before venturing forth into the forex market.

The forex market becomes a source of information for position traders. When you are a position trader, you make use of the movement of other financial instruments — such as forex — to understand the value of your stock.

Chapter 4: Fundamental Analysis

Before you decide to analyze the stocks, you might come across a choice. You have to decide whether you would like to pick fundamental analysis or technical analysis.

Both forms of analysis have the same purpose: they are techniques that are used by traders and investors around the world to understand the stock market and make better decisions.

However, the key difference between them is how they operate and the type of data that they utilize to provide you with insights.

- On one hand, fundamental analysis aims to predict the prices of the stocks based on various industrial, economic, and company data and statistics. It also uses interests and dividends to make predictions about the stocks. It is almost like taking a birds' eye approach to data and statistics.

- On the other hand, you have technical analysis. This form of analysis focuses on the activity within the market. It uses internal market data to allow you to make your strategies and predictions.

But apart from the methods that are used by fundamental and technical analysis, there are other notable differences as well. Let us look at some of them below.

Factor	Fundamental Analysis	Technical Analysis
Approach	Using various economic factors to predict the value of securities	Using the movements of prices and patterns on charts to predict the value of securities
Price Movements	It is focused on predicting the long-term movement of securities. This is why	People who are using technical analysis are aiming for short-term price movements. They

	most investors who are using fundamental analysis are doing so to invest for a long-term. Because of this, they need to understand the numerous factors that could affect the movement of prices.	have strategies in place to buy and sell securities in the near future. A technical analysis becomes vital for securities such as forex, where transactions are conducted in the short-term.
Value of Share s	A fundamental analyst believes that there is an intrinsic value for each security and usually purchases that security when it falls below the intrinsic value. Using the same intrinsic value, he sells the security when its price goes above that value. Through this method, he or she makes a profit. Of course, finding out that intrinsic value means he has to use all the data provided by fundamental analysis.	A technical analyst believes in the fact that stocks don't have any particular value. He or she is of the opinion that only the forces of demand and supply can truly affect the prices of the stocks. THis is why, they avoid placing any particular value on the stock and simply base their decision on the direction in which the market is moving.

Trends	In fundamental analysis, people believe that there is no hope for using past trends or look for any sort of fluctuations in the prices.	Technical analysts are of the opinion that past trends may repeat over time. They use historical data and chart information to find out if there is a possibility that there is a repeat of a past trend.
Assumptions	Fundamental analysts do not make any assumptions. They review their decisions based on the information that they have gathered from various sources that we talked about earlier.	Technical analysts make certain assumptions. One of the reasons for this is the idea that past trends can repeat again.
Decisions	To a fundamental analyst, there are numerous factors that are used to come to a decision. In many ways, the decision of a fundamental analyst are based on his or her subjective opinions.	Analysts do not have any personal view of things. they are solely dependent on the direction of the market. To them, the market is the one giving the opinions.

Chang es	Because fundamental analysis is based on long-term strategies and patterns, the indicators change less frequently than technical analysis. Usually, fundamental analysis indicators change on a quarterly basis.	Short-term strategies require frequent changes in indicators. You will notice that it takes weeks, days, and sometimes even mere hours to notice changes in indicators.

Need for Fundamental Analysis in Position Trading

Some of you might think that having technical analysis tools will suffice for making decisions. After all, you have everything you require to focus on the factors in the market. You feel that paying attention to the market is more important than considering what economic factors influence a company or a stock.

When you use fundamental analysis, though, you are not merely aiming to make predictions. You are looking at the overall performance and health of any company. Remember the passage regarding Nokia that we looked at earlier. If one were to simply use technical analysis, then the bigger picture of the rock might be ignored to look at the immediate position of the stock. However, if one had used fundamental analysis, then they would look at the stock from a broader perspective.

That is where fundamental analysis becomes important. It tries to answer some of the important questions that you might have about a company or stock, such as:

- Is it really true that the company is going to see a rise in revenue?

- Is the company capable of making an actual profit?

- Does the company stand a chance to beat the competitors in the future?

Like the questions above, fundamental analysis tackles many other queries that are important to understand where the market is going.

Apart from that, here are some other advantages of fundamental analysis.

Discovering Future Movement of Prices

Since you are using position trading to work on long-term strategies, you might need to have an idea of how the prices might move in the future. This movement will then help you decide whether you would like to invest more in a stock or whether you should be prepared to sell it. The one way you are going to gain an understanding of future price movements is through fundamental analysis.

Fair Value

Fundamental analysis plays an important role in finding out the company's fair value. This fair value helps you understand the company's present financial standing. This, in turn, lets you know the amount that has to be paid between parties if the stock of the company is sold in the market.

Management Evaluation

When you use fundamental analysis, you are also evaluating the management and trying to find out more about their internal decisions. It is similar to the forex market, where you evaluate an entire country so that you can understand what is going to happen to its currency. By knowing about the management of a company, you might be able to predict the direction the stocks might take as a position trader.

Competitive Advantage

When you use fundamental analysis, you are also finding out if the company you are focusing on has the ability to beat its competitors. This factor becomes important in determining whether the value of the stock you are holding will increase or decrease in the future. This is why, you need to ask yourself, "Is the company capable of growing to such a point that it can beat the competition?"

Financial Strength

It is always nice to see that a company is growing. Does that mean the company is financially strong, though? Is the company capable of paying off all its debts on time? One of the mistakes that traders make is that they do not conduct more research on the company before purchasing their stock. They look at the company's current value and position and think that it is poised for success. They miss out on seeing the financial capabilities and strengths of the company.

When you use fundamental analysis, you enter the market with all the cards on the table. You are not hoping that something will happen. You have an understanding of what might happen based on information available to you. In other words, your level or certainty increases.

Understanding Important Concepts

At this point, we are clear that fundamental analysis is important for position trading. But while you are working with fundamental analysis, you might come across certain terms that could stop you in your tracks and make you wonder, "Wait, what is this? What is it trying to tell me?"

Earnings Per Share

We use earnings per share to measure how much profit a company has earned. Typically, you might begin to notice that companies release their earnings per share data on a quarterly or yearly basis.

Essentially, earnings per share is a portion of the profits of the company that is allotted to each outstanding share.

Let us say that a company has generated a net income of $20 million. It now has to pay off the dividends of the preferred shareholders. Assume that the amount for preferred shareholders is $2 million and further assume that it now has 10 million shares that are outstanding in the first quarter of the year. In the next quarter, it has about 12 million shares that are outstanding. Based on the information provided, here is how we will calculate the earnings per share.

We first remove the amount already paid to the preferred shareholders.

That would be:

$20 million - $2 million = $18 million

We can now use the remaining $18 million to measure the earnings per share.

Since it has 10 million shares outstanding in one quarter and 12 million in another, then it has an average of 11 million shares outstanding. An important note to make here. WE are calculating average to only measure the earnings per share of the company. We are not using it to show how many shares the company has to pay. If a company has 10 million shares outstanding, it has to pay all 10 million shares. The same rule applies if it has 12 million shares as well.

The next part is fairly simple. We take the amount it has right now — which would be $18 million — and then divide it by the number of shares outstanding.

Therefore, $18 million divided by 11 million shares.

This gives a value of $1.63.

In other words, the company's earnings per share is $1.63. In other words, it has earned $1.63 for each share investment made into the company.

Price-to-Earnings Ratio

The price-to-earnings (P/E) ratio is a way to evaluate the value of a company that uses its earnings per share to measure its current share price. In other words, you are establishing a relation between the company's stock prices and the earnings per share.

The P/E ratio is used widely to gain a better understanding of the value of a company. Earnings are vital to understand the health of a company because investors need to know the degree of portability of the company in the present and the degree of profitability it will attain in the future. Both of these factors help the investor understand how to use his or her money effectively.

Debt to Equity

The debt-to-equity (D/E) ratio is calculated by taking the total liabilities of the company and dividing it by the company's shareholder equity. One uses this ratio to find out how much financing the company has received from investors and creditors. When it is higher, then it means that the company has received a major part of its financing from creditors (for example, from banks). It's investor financing (from the issue of shares) is lower.

How is this ratio used?

If there is a high debt to equity ratio, then the company could be considered as a financial risk to many traders. This is because of the fact that when companies have high loans, then the losses suffered by the companies if they do not meet those loans are higher.

Traders do not want to risk their investments on a company that cannot maintain its debts.

Return on Equity

The return on equity is a ratio that measures profitability. This profitability measures the ability of the company to create profits from the investments made the shareholders in the company. In other words, traders can use this ratio to find out how much profit each dollar they invest in the company generates.

This ratio is not measured by the company. Rather, it is used by the investors to gauge the level of success of a company and how much they are going to receive for the investment they pour into the company. In other words, it is a way to evaluate how much profits trades can make and whether they are capable of getting their money back.

Cash Flow Ratio

All companies have certain degree of liabilities.

But the question is, "What is happening to those liabilities?"

This is what the cash flow ratio aims to answer. It simply aims to find out how well the company is able to manage its liabilities with the cash that is flowing into it through various operations and assets. This helps measure the liquidity of the company.

As you might have guessed, a cash flow ratio lets you know if the company is capable of managing its liabilities. This means, can it pay back its shareholders easily or is it going to face some roadblocks in that area? With that knowledge in hand, you are able to make more sound investment decisions.

As you might have guessed, a cash flow ratio lets you know if the company is capable of managing its liabilities. Meaning, can it pay back its shareholders easily or is it going to face some roadblocks in that area? With that knowledge in hand, you are able to make more sound investment decisions.

Chapter 5: Position Trading Indicators

Before you decide to analyze the stocks, you might come across a choice. You have to decide whether you would like to pick fundamental analysis or technical analysis.

Both forms of analysis have the same purpose: they are techniques that are used by traders and investors around the world to understand the stock market and make better decisions.

When new traders enter into the market, they are faced with understanding trade indicators. There is just so much information in front of you that making heads or tails of it might seem like a daunting task. In fact, many traders skip using the indicators and hope that they are able to gain their information from other sources.

But avoiding the indicators is not going to solve anything. Rather, it might just make your decisions riskier.

Let us start with technical indicators.

When you enter into the market, you are going to notice numerous technical indicators. You might ponder about which one you should consider or if all of them are important to you in some way. You look at each indicator and try to find out what they are trying to say in the hopes that one of them might make more sense to you than the others. But that is not the right way to go about things. There is an easier approach.

All you need to know is that most technical indicators give you the same set of information in different ways.

Many traders have already been in your position. They have experienced the same mistakes that you have made. This is why, it is better to learn from past mistakes.

Before we delve deeper into technical analysis, let us first try to understand two concepts that are commonly used in technical analysis. These two concepts are part of the chart patterns that you analyze.

Support

Support usually occurs during a downward trend in the price levels. As the prices continue to go down, there can be a pause in their progress because of a sudden surge in demand. As the price of securities continue to drop, an increase in the demand for the securities increase. The increase in demand acts as a support line for the ashes.

In a similar manner, a resistance occurs when there is an increase in the sell-off of stocks as the price is increasing.

Once traders have identified a certain "area" of of support or resistance, then it helps them with finding out where they would like to enter or exit the trade. When the price reaches a particular point that is either a support or resistance, then one of the two situations will occur: the price will hit the support or resistant point and bounce back or it might continue on its trajectory, in which case a new support or resistance point is established.

How does this work with trades?

Simple. Many trades are made on the prediction that the prices will not pass the support or resistant points. Other traders make predictions on the fact that prices will cross the aforementioned points. Either way, how you predict the market can determine whether it works in your favor or against you.

So, how does one decide the support and resistance levels? Let's use an example to find out.

We now have a trader named Andrew who saw that over the past few months, the price of these tock has not risen above $51. It has reached the $51 point repeatedly, but it has not managed to cross that mark yet. In such a scenario, $51 will be considered as the resistance point. This is made on the belief that the price won't go beyond that point. Based on this, traders can start making predictions on the price. If they decide that there is a possibility that the price might cross the resistant point, then they can modify their strategies accordingly.

Novice traders often make the mistake of selling into support because they begin to panic about the situation of the stock. They think that they are going to make a loss and make rash decisions. A smart trader will be looking for this opportunity and buy what the new trader has sold. Eventually, when the chart shows the price reaching into resistance, the experienced trader sells their stock and ends up making a lot of money. Novice traders also end up buying into support, thinking that the prices may rise even further in the future. This strategy is not based on any knowledge of the market but a general understanding of the mechanisms of support and resistance. Selling into support and buying into resistance are not always the most prudent courses of action to take.

Hence, it helps to understand various parts of a technical analysis.

200-Day EMA

One of the technical indicators that you might notice is popular in the market is the 200-day Moving Average or 200-day EMA.

It is calculated by taking the average of a security's (in this case, a stock's) closing price across the last 200 days.

In other words, you take the average from Day 1, Day 2, Day 3, and all the way to Day 200. You then add the numbers together and finally divide that number by 200. Typically, you won't have to perform the calculations on your own as the platform you are using will provide you with the 200-day EMA by itself. However, in case you decide that perhaps you trust only yourself, then you now have the formula.

When you look at the 200-day EMA broadly, then you might automatically assume that as the average gets higher, the more it enters the bullish market. After all, an increase in the average means things are looking good right?

This is where novice traders make mistakes. They end up taking everything at face value without realizing how the market works. When there are high readings, it is considered as a warning by smart traders. While novice traders might think of this as an opportunity to buy stocks, smart traders realize that a big change is just looming over the horizon. When there are high readings, it means that traders are overly optimistic. There are not many new buyers in the market. This eventually causes the market to reverse and begin to head in the downward direction faster than you can say, "Wait, what just happened?"

50-Day EMA

A 50-day Moving Average or 50-day EMA is similar to the 200-day EMA. The only difference is that you are calculating the average over the course of a 50-day period rather than take into consideration 200 days. Even when using just 50 days, one has to realize that just because the average is getting higher and higher, it does not mean that the market it bullish. Try and find out how quickly the average is rising. Ask yourself if this makes any sense to you. Do not only look for optimistic results as that is a calamitous approach to take in a stock market.

Stochastic RSI

The Stochastic RSI is an indicator that makes use of the relative strength index (RSI) values. A Stochastic oscillator formula is used on the RSI values in order to get results that fall into the range of zero to a hundred.

- An RSI is an index that measures the momentum of price. This allows traders to evaluate those situations where the stock has been overbought or oversold.

- An oscillator, on the other hand, is an analysis tool that shifts between two extreme points. By using these points, it can create a trend indicator.

When you combine both factors, then you can understand that the Stochastic oscillator helps in finding out whether a particular RSI value is oversold or overbought. It appears by placing values between two oscillation points, zero and hundred.

The Stochastic RSI is using properties of two different factors to create an indicator that is highly sensitive to the price changes in the market. This is why most traders use it to evaluate the historical performance of a particular stock rather than use it for a general price analysis.

In other words, you are looking at the bigger picture instead of just what is happening to the price right now.

Getting a Clearer Picture of Technical Analysis

By using technical analysis, you are using a certain analysis discipline to perform an evaluation on the investments you own. This allows you to see trading opportunities and are usually depicted as patterns and trends on charts.

Because technical analysts believe that past trends can have a big impact on the price movements in the future, they are consciously looking at historical data to notice any patterns that they can use in their analysis.

Now, one of the things that you might wonder when looking at the charts during technical analysis is what exactly drives the patterns and trends. Is there an unknown force that no one can see that is secretly influencing the analysis? Is this an indication that the Illuminati exists and that they are influencing the stock markets secretly?

Well, before the paranoia sets in, let us clear up some misconceptions. All the numbers, patterns, and trends that you see on the charts are not arbitrarily decided. They are based on the decisions, predictions, and actions of human beings.

Let us take a small example.

When traders are optimistic about the market, they react accordingly. This causes the demand in the market to increase, which eventually causes the prices to increase. When you are using your 200-day EMA, you might notice that things are looking good. But does that mean it will continue to stay good? Eventually, there might be a downward trajectory of the prices in the market. Even the downward direction of the price is determined by human beings as well, as there are fewer buyers in the market. When you begin to understand the human logic that guides most of the patterns and trends on the charts, you realize that they become more predictable.

Suddenly, you see the charts with more clarity. You do not get intimidated by the big numbers and complex patterns either. You realize that it is all about cause and reaction. A reaction has a particular cause and you can usually trace back the patterns to that cause. Now, you are probably feeling more comfortable approaching charts. That is good. After all, you do need to maintain a clear head if you would like to know more and start making important financial decisions.

When you first start looking at charts for technical analysis, then you might notice that there are options to choose the time frame. You can choose anywhere from one-minute time frame to a monthly time analysis to even years. The time frames that you choose to analyze depends entirely on your trading style. There are some popular time frames that many traders typically use, including

- 5 minutes

- 15 minutes

- Hourly

- 4 hours

- Daily

For example, if you are trading in the short-term, then you might consider using the 5-minute, 15-minute, or even daily charts to perform your analysis. However, if you are a position trader, then using small time frame is not going to help you out a lot. Besides, it might just bombard you with so much data that you are going to spend hours, and maybe even days, to go through all that data. It does not seem practical at all.

Rather, if you are focusing on long-term trades, you might want to analyze your data in month-by-month increments or even yearly data (if you are planning to keep you position open for long).

Another thing that you might notice — apart from the option to choose the time frame — is the option to use different kinds of charts for the purpose of technical analysis.

Let us look at some of the tools and indicators that one can use for technical analysis.

Trendline Indicator

Trendlines are a popular form of indicators in technical analysis. This makes sense since technical analysis focuses on the fact that the market can show trends (which is why they focus on past data in order to spot future trends).

You may not be able to find trends in the short run. However, as you look at charts over a period of days or weeks or even months, you might begin to notice certain patterns in the charts. These patterns can, in turn, be used to make predictions and strategies.

Hence, when you use a trendline indicator, you can get a possible direction for the price action. While the direction is also a form of prediction (as you might never be sure of what happens in the future), it is not entirely a guess. This is because that direction your find will be based on data and not random factors.

Support and Resistance

We have already understood what support and resistance can do for your technical analysis. One thing to reiterate here is that when a price action breaks the present support or resistant levels, then it usually continues onto the next or bounces away from the point it was heading for and move in the opposite direction. Make sure you are aware of this when you are planning to buy or sell stocks.

Moving Average Indicators

We have already seen two types of moving averages: the 200-day EMA and 50-day EMA. In the grand scheme of things, it won't matter much if you do not have the required data to measure either the 200-day or the 50-day EMA. It is only when you have the measurements for either of the EMAs that you are able to get a clear picture of the market. Additionally, you can also use the 100-day EMA and the 500-day EMA as well. Both of these indicators, when combined with the 50-day and 200-day EMAs, are going to explain the market to you properly. Never think that one particular EMA as the main source of information. Try and analyze the market using different approaches and see what valuable information you can find out about your stocks.

Bottom Line

Here is an important thing to remember: this book can help you find out about different technical analysis available to you. You might even be introduced to the concepts behind those analysis methods. However, you cannot use the concepts you have learnt here to perform technical analysis in detail. If you would like to learn more, then you need to delve into books that are specially made to help you navigate the various components of technical analysis.

If you would like to train yourself in the technical analysis methods, then you need to get yourself a book that will not only serve as a primer to the analysis but take you through the steps to learn more about it.

I personally recommend the book *Trend Trading For Dummies* by Barry Burns. The book is easy to browse through and provides you with step-by-step methods work with technical analysis.

I have noticed that many people are drawn towards *Technical Analysis for Dummies*. While many people might think that the two books can be interchangeable and that getting either of those books will help, do note that there is a vast difference between the books. For one, *Trend Trading for Dummies* slowly eases you into the concepts of technical analysis and gain mastery over it.

Now that we have gone over technical analysis, it is finally time to step into the realm of momentum stocks.

Chapter 6: Identifying Momentum Stocks

You have understood what tools you are going to require when entering the market. You have understood certain concepts that will help you when navigating the market. Now it is time to finally understand how to identify certain stocks. Most importantly, we are going to identify momentum stocks.

Still, what is momentum investing?

Momentum Investing

The main idea behind momentum investing is to capitalize on a particular market trend that is occurring continuously. It means that when securities start showing upward trends, then you are going to go long and when they start showing downward trends, then you are going to go short.

Now, you are probably wondering, "What does going long and going short mean?" Surely, it has got nothing to do with height.

It does not.

Going long can also be understood as having a long position. This means that you own a particular security. When someone goes long, it refers to the act of continuing to own the security in the hopes that the value of the stock will rise in the future.

The opposite of going long is going short. When you are going short, you are holding a short position, which is indicated by the sale of a stock that you do not personally own. This means that the investor borrows a certain stock and sells it back to the lender. This is done in the hopes that the price of the stock will drop, and the investor can buy it at a low price.

One of the strategies used by investors in momentum investing is moving averages. The investors use one average that is shorter than the other average.

For example, the two averages one can consider could be the 50-day or 200-day moving average. When the 50-day average crosses the 200-day average, then it gives an indication to the investor to buy stocks. In the same way, if the 50-day average falls below the 200-day average, then the trader has to go for a sell strategy.

Momentum Stocks

One of the first steps that you will be taking is identifying the momentum stocks. You can use many criteria in order to identify these stocks. These criteria can be used on their own or in combination with other criteria. The main goal is to identify those stocks that are really experiencing a momentum in the market.

One trick that can be used here is entering the search criteria into a stock scanner. This will help you narrow down the potential list of stocks to find those that have momentum. Once you have the stocks ready, you can analyze them even more before you decide to trade using any one of them.

By using the below criteria, you will be able to find stocks that can easily go in an upward trajectory and increase in value by 30% or even 100% in just 3 months. Of course, you will have to do the legwork of researching more about the stocks you have with you and figuring out just which one those socks is going to give you the return you are looking for.

Earnings Growth

A common characteristic that you will notice in most, if not all, momentum stocks is that they are frequently showing a growth in their revenue and earnings per share. In many cases, momentums stocks tend to outperform the predictions set down by the analysts. So, how can you find out these stocks? Simple. You look for those stocks that have shown an increase in earnings per share from one quarter to another. You should ideally make sure that increases have happened in the past year. It would be even more advantageous for you if you can find stocks that have also shown an increase in their earnings per share in the most recent quarter when you compare it to the same quarter last year.

For example, if you notice that the earnings per share in Q1 (or first quarter) of a company in the year 2019 is higher than Q1 of the company in the year 2018, then you are probably looking at a momentum stock. But do not just jump to conclusions about the stock. Make sure that you are checking the growth in Q2, Q3, and Q4 of 2018 as well to get a better picture of the performance of the stock.

High Returns

In the short-term, it is quite easy to spot a momentum stock. There is no challenge in that endeavor. However, it then becomes rather difficult when you would like to know true momentum stocks. One can go about that by analyzing the prices of the stocks that are yielding high returns over the past three or six months. In fact, make sure that you measure the yield for the past year as well. You should compare the yields that you discover to some of the popular indices in the world (such as S&P 500). You should then see if the yield generated by your stock is higher than the indices that you are comparing the stock to.

New Highs

Another trait of momentum sock is that they are constantly setting new highs for themselves. It may not happen constantly, but over a period of time, you might notice that the company is always aiming to match the highs that they created and then break those highs., eventually creating a new target. This shows that the stock is on a constant upward trend. Some of these stocks might even increase by 30% or even 100% in a relatively short span of 3 months. Of course, the trick is to find these stocks in the market. Remember that you should never assume anything when you can find information about it. The key motto that you should follow is: *The more you learn, the more you earn.*

If you are able to find information about something, then make sure that you have acquired that information. Do not simply assume something and hope that it is true. You might come across certain scenarios where you are not able to get any information. That is completely alright because you lack information. It was not because you did not try to get it, but it was unavailable to you for a reason.

Important Tips for Momentum Traders

Entering the market can be a daunting task. You have to figure out most of the way yourself. Even if you are going through hundreds of lessons and information, you are the one to eventually take action.

In fact, there is a big difference between knowing what you have to do and actually taking action to do it. Let us look at the example of practice sessions. Many traders use practice sessions and trading simulators to practice their trading game. They come up with a strategy that seems to work every time they use their simulation. However, once they begin to trade in real, they give up all their strategies and simply go in another direction entirely.

They had a winning strategy, but when it came to trade in real, the completely ignored that strategy.

This is always what happens when you have all the information and lessons. You might think you are prepared but when you enter into a trade, then everything changes.

Thus, here are some important tips that you can take with you when entering a momentum trade.

Do Not Get Attached to Stocks

A losing stock is a losing stock. Do not get attached to it and hope that it is going to change directions in the future. Do not try to bounce back with that particular stock. Sometimes, it is better to cut losses and try a different avenue than stick to one particular stock than watch as your capital continues to dwindle away.

Do Not Try to Choose Bottoms and Tops

You are not here to identify the top of the trend or the bottom of the trend. Those are just assumptions. You are here to look at the trend and see where it is going to take you.

Make sure that you are sticking to the trend. In order to identify tops and bottoms, you will have to go through another set of analysis. Which is why, stick to the knowledge that you have about momentum stocks.

Be Confident

This might seem like an obvious trait for traders to have. After all, why go into trading is one is not confident about the trade? However, there are many traders who do lose their confidence as soon as they start looking at the numbers and the trends.

It is easy to get overwhelmed by all the date surrounding you. But the key thing to remember is that you need to focus on what you know. Do not try and take in all the information at once. That could overload your mind and even change your opinions about your trade. Simply look at the things you already know. Try to get your bearings straight. If there are numerous information available, then try to start with the one that makes the most sense to you. When you have identified one, then move on to the other. As you solve each part of the puzzle, you gain more confidence in your abilities and your knowledge.

Know When You Are Wrong

Do not cover your mistakes by trying to do something else. When you are wrong, take a moment to admit that you are wrong and see what happened. Analyze the mistake and see what went wrong and when.

As soon as you admit that you are wrong, you will stop wasting time on a trade that is not yielding the results that you want.

Remember That Results Take Time

You are a position trader. Do not be hasty when you do not see results for some time. You are playing for the long run. So, make sure you have your eye on the price and wait for the trade to pick up. If you notice that eventually, the trade is not working out for you, plan some strategies so that you know how much losses you are willing to bear before you pull out of the stock.

The Essential Concept

Professional traders are not impatient. They are calculating, and they wait for their turn to strike. Because of that, they typically buy after a wave of selling has occurred. This allows them to buy at the conditions that are suitable to them. Similarly, they sell after a wave of buying has occurred. During both the aforementioned scenarios, professional traders make sure that they have the right conditions to make a move in the market.

You see, when novice traders see a rise in the market, they react to it immediately. They think that they are going to miss out on some big action and decide to buy stocks. After all, buying them now and selling them later when the price is even higher, right? It seems like simple logic. Only, in the world of trading, nothing can be boiled down to simple logic. Professionals usually wait to see what happens in the market. Most of the time, they are selling their stocks and gaining what profits they can. This way, when the market eventually goes down, they can start buying stocks at the cheap. Rinse and repeat, and you have a strong strategy there. Of course, it is not always that simple, but it gives you an idea of what you should be doing when you notice a particular trend: do not look for the obvious.

Now let's take a look at one of the greatest momentum stock trades of all time.

George Soros

George Soros is often considered as one of the most successful traders in recent history. What elevated him to that position was a single trade that he conducted on September 16 1992 which would reap him an astonishing amount.

In the 1992, England was part of the European Exchange Rate Mechanism. This was a fixed-rate system that also included numerous European nations. The other countries realized that the value of the British Pound was high, and they put the pressure on England to devalue the currency so that it matches the strength of the other countries in the system. England, on the other hand, resisted the pressure for as long as it could, but eventually decided to float its currency. Soros saw what was going on and leveraged his firm against the pound, shorting it continously. Ultimately the Bank of England caved in, and stopped artificially propping up the currency, and eventually withdrawing it from the ERM. Betting against the Bank of England resulted in Soros netting an incredible $1 billion in a single day and cementing his reputation as the world's #1 currency speculator.

Benefit of 50-Day and 200-Day EMAs

As we saw earlier, the 50-day and 200-day EMAs are convenient if you would like to place a strategy to find out when you would like to buy or sell stocks. You use one average, which is the 200-day EMA average to place points on the charts. When you notice that the 50-day EMA crosses the 200-day EMA in a particular manner, then you can decide what you would like to do with your stocks.

In fact, in the world of trading, when the 50-day EMA goes past the 200-day EMA, then the situation is called a "cross." There are two types of crosses: the golden cross and the death cross. Understand both these crosses will help you plan your trading game better. When the 50-day moving average increases above the 200-day moving average, then the situation called a golden cross and is usually considered as the sign of a bullish market. If the 50-day moving average dips below the 200-day moving average, the situation is called a death cross and is usually indicative of a bearish market.

Through such simple measures, you will be able to get a clearer idea of the market. This allows you to predict properly if the market is a bull or bear market.

Getting to know more about the 50-day and 200-day moving average is going to help you in your trades. Consider them as your trading friends, guiding you on the right path.

Chapter 7: Hot Sector Mania

Upon entering the stock market, you might find yourself wondering what sector you should tackle first. The idea of choosing the right sector becomes a daunting task because you know that there are so many options available to you.

You need to ding the right sector.

You need to find the hot sector.

Now, what is a sector?

Understanding Sectors

Think of sectors are the various sections in a library. You have the non-fiction section, fiction, biographies, history, science, and so on.

In a similar way, the stock market gets broken down into various sectors such as healthcare, energy, defense, and so on.

Typically, there are 11 major sectors that are used in stock exchanges and are the ones that comprise the economies of the world.

- Financial

- Consumer Discretionary

- Consumer Staples

- Utilities

- Energy

- Healthcare

- Telecom

- Industrials

- Technology

- Materials

- Real Estate

What exactly does recognizing a hot sector does for you?

If you can identify that one sector that seems to be on the rise, then you can invest in that sector while it is still in its growth phase. It gives traders the opportunity to work with something over the course of 3 to 12 months. Eventually, it allows them to utilize short-term trading opportunities.

How to Use Hot Sectors

Certain sectors perform better than others. Typically, the top performing sectors keep changing. If we look at the market when it is heading higher, then we need to identify which sectors is causing the increase in the market. Ideally, we should be buying stocks from the sector that is in the top position. These are usually those sectors that are performing better than the other actors in the market.

When you want to pick the hot sectors, then you have to evaluate the market from various time frames. You should not stick to just a few time frames as you might not get the most accurate results. After all, every sector shows an increase at some point in time or between a short period of time. In other words, you should be looking at sectors that are not just performing well now or a few months in the past, but also over an even longer period.

When you analyze the data, you might come across a few sectors that can be identified as the hot sectors.

Additionally, always keep a lookout on the latest news as well. You might be able to glean some valuable information and tips about what sectors have been performing really well over the course of time.

Let us look at some of the hot sectors in the market in the year 2019 so that we can get an idea of what to look out for when it comes to hot sectors.

Healthcare

The year 2019 has shown a growth in the healthcare sector. In fact, it has been performing well in the last 10 years, showing the stability of the sector. You can probably expect to use a good short-term strategy in the healthcare sector. In 2018, healthcare was the top performing sector, and while it might not have the top spot right now, it is still among the top performing sectors.

Industrial

The industrial sector is also booming. However, there are many components to the industrial sector, so choosing the right component becomes important. In this case (and for the year 2019), you should be looking at those industries that focus on pollution control, such as waste management companies. Since the concern for the planet's safety is on the rise and there is greater demand to protect the natural resources of the Earth, the demand for waste management companies is on the rise. One such example can be US Ecology (ECOL), which has been trading in the midrange for its 52nd week, maintaining consistency, and not showing any dip. Currently, the value of the stock has increased by 1.88% and is trading for $63.99.

Technology

If explosive yet volatile growth is your MO, you cannot typically go wrong with the technology sector. You have lots of options for technology, from computing to mobile technology to space tech. You can always explore on or the other segments within the sector. In 2019, the big tech companies like Apple (AAPL) are still showing signs of growth. Currently, the stock value of Apple has increased by 4.59% and stands at $218.36. There are recommendations to go into other different segments like credit card providers and software manufacturers.

Consumer Discretionary

This sector is still showing a rise. However, be warned as many of the companies have been hit by what is known as the "Amazon effect." The online retail behemoth is still posing a threat to other companies, even though its stock value dropped by 0.37%. Currently the value of Amazon (AMZN) is $1891.53. However, there are still opportunities in the market. One only has to look at those companies that are trying to use innovating methods to lure customers to come to their stores. If you have been noticing an increase in shop visits in one of the stores despite how Amazon has affected the market, then you should consider investing in that particular store.

Let us look at some other examples of companies and sectors that were either at the top of the market or are currently topping the markets.

Dotcom Boom

Yahoo!

One of the finest examples of the dotcom boom was Yahoo! The company was initially founded by two Stanford students, David Filo, and Jerry Yang. The main idea was to create a web page that listed other websites that are interesting to the public. By the time the year 1994 arrived, Yahoo! had over hundreds of websites linked to it and was receiving an average of 1,000 page visits every week. By late 1994, the website was receiving almost 50,000 hits per day on their website. In 1996, Yahoo! had generated a revenue of $19.1 million. Their growth would continue to increase in the next year as well. After a round of investment, Apple created its IPO. On the first day the company went public, their stocks were traded at $33 per share. They were aiming for a market capitalization of $315 million. They received a market capitalization of $866 million.

Eventually, Yahoo! entered the dotcom bubble in the years 1998-2000. After that, there were many failed investments, such as the purchase of Flickr and del.icio.us. However none of them could stop the decline in Yahoo!'s value. Once Google and Facebook entered the picture, the platform struggled to offer anything of value. The two new giants would soon dominate the market with superior offerings and better services.

The result was that Yahoo! got sold to the highest bidder, which so happens to be Verizon. The price is $4.8 billion.

If that seemed like a lot to you, then you have to consider the fact that during the dotcom bubble, Yahoo!'s value was $125 billion.

Within just 12 years, it was sold for less than 4% of its original value.

Cisco

Cisco is another company that went through the dotcom bubble. In 2011, the company announced that it would lay off 5,000 employees and even sell off a manufacturing plant in Mexico.

During the dotcom bubble, Cisco's position in the markets was so strong that it even passed Microsoft to become one of the most valuable companies in the world.

The problem with Cisco is one of growth. You see, Cisco had already reached its highest growth potential. However, investors were always seeking to see more growth. Eventually, Cisco acquired Linksys in 2003 and went on to make other acquisitions further down the line. But it was obvious. Cisco had reached its prime value during the dotcom bubble.

Eventually, the 2008 market crash hit Cisco hard. They had privately laid off 2,000 people in 2009. After trying to venture in the market for video, it made some failed investments that eventually came to haunt it in the future.

Currently, the company is losing market shares but has been managing to hold on. As of 2019, it has been showing a rise in tis stock value (by an increase of 0.27%). However, the stock itself is valued at just $56.63.

Cryptocurrency

Bitcoin

For a 6 month period in late 2017 and early 2018, it seemed impossible to go 5 minutes without hearing about Bitcoin. A meteoric rise, compared by some analysts to the Dutch tulip mania in the 17th Century, was followed by a spectacular crash in the first half of 2017. Since then, things have calmed down somewhat and the world's premiere cryptocurrency has undergone somewhat of a quiet resurgence. In 2019, Bitcoin has shown a rise of nearly 200%. One of the reasons for this is the process known as "the halvening." In this process, Bitcoin miners will only receive half rewards.

Who are Bitcoin miners? Essentially, they are groups of people who combine their computing power in order to split the Bitcoin between the participants. This happens when the groups combined computing power is able to create new Bitcoins. These new Bitcoins will then be shared by the members of the group.

Whatever the reason may be, Bitcoin is definitely showing a rise. Whether Ethereum will soon overtake it is something that has to be seen.

Ethereum

Ethereum is the second most popular cryptocurrency in the world after Bitcoin. Some people compare the idea of buying Ethereum to purchasing a stock of Apple back when it was still growing out of a garage. expect that it might grow tremendously over the years. But due to the volatility of the market, that has to be seen.

Some analysts are predicting that that price of Ethereum will increase to nearly $2,500 this year. And this rise will continue on to the next year as well. Others are predicting that the value of Ethereum will overtake that of Bitcoin. We are still in the early stages of predictions so one cannot say what might happen by the year 2020. Others are less optimistic and have likened Ethereum to Tesla, in that it is an innovative technology, but one which may never be financially feasible.

Ripple

Ripple is a cryptocurrency that is relatively newer in the market. However, it has been showing considerable growth in recent years.

Many analysts predict that Ripple will increase its value by nearly hundredfold by the time it reaches the next bull cycle. Once again, while the cryptocurrency is definitely on the rise, it only remains to be seen if it will show a sudden upward trajectory in the future.

New Technology

Twitter

The social media company has been seeing a rise in its stock market value recently. After its daily users rose to around 139 million, the stock rose more than 5% as of June 26th. Currently, the company is showing further growth as the stock, as of July 31st, shows an increase of 4.78%. The current stock value is at $42.77.

Apple

Apple (AAPL) has always shown a growth. As we had seen earlier, the stock value of Apple has increased by 4.59% and stands at $218.36. The company has always shown improvements in the past and is continuing to do so.

Tesla

After a rough 2018, Tesla has been on the increase recently. By showing an increase of 1.53% as of July 31st, Tesla has a stock value of $245.71. With new funding from the company and its special interest in space exploration (and the trip to Mars of course), the company had garnered the attention (and even the imagination) of people around the world. Now, it only depends on how well it can perform in the coming years.

Marijuana Boom

With the laws against marijuana becoming more lenient, the industry has been seeing a boom in recent years. Here are some entities to look out for.

Canopy Growth Corporation

One of the most talked about stocks in 2018, and which began receiving mainstream coverage in 2019, the marijuana industry is seeing a boom that picked up in recent years. Despite that, you can see the effect of it on various corporations, starting with the Canopy Growth Corporation. One of the bigger players in the market, and one of the few stocks listed on the NYSE, Canopy had a rough past few months due to previous overvaluation. At the time of writing it trades at around the $32 mark and many analysts have set a buy price between $27 and $33 in the short term.

Altria

Overall, Altria Group Inc. has not been showing a growth recently. But that does not mean that it has a bad value in the market.

Formula Companies

Starbucks

The historical data of Starbucks has shown only one thing: the company has always managed to perform well and show an increase over the years. In the year 2015, the stock was traded at around $45 to $50. Now, you can see an increase in the stock value as it is now being traded at approximately $96.

In fact, one can say that this year has shown an incredible increase in the value of Starbucks. However, this growth has always been the case for the company. It has been on the rise since early 2010 and kept progressing upwards. This trend looks set to continue even after the resignation of long time CEO Howard Schultz, due to Starbucks global expansion into countries which have not traditionally had a big coffee culture like China and India. Starbucks has a unique position in this sense because they are perceived as a luxury good, but at a price which is affordable even to middle class citizens of third world countries.

Amazon

The rise of Amazon is big. In fact, currently the company has such a powerful position that it is dominating the market and overshadowing the other retail companies. The entire phenomenon has been dubbed the "Amazon effect." However, there are many companies that are adapting themselves to this effect. Those companies are making progress despite the presence of the giant retailer.

McDonald's

Another company that has been showing historical growth is McDonald's. Although the current valuation is recovering from a dip, it has always been showing growth projections from one year to the next. This makes McDonald's stock a valuable stock to have. While there has been competition from other brands such as Burger King and Wendy's (especially since the latter two brands have also been growing in popularity), McDonald's has managed to keep the top position when it comes to comparing with its competitors.

Final Words

When you look at the stock value of the above companies, then you might be thinking that there is no way that anything could affect their prices.

Take the value of Starbucks as an example. It has shown a sudden increase in value. In fact, if you look at how the value has been increasing, then one can say that there has been a spike in the value. But does that mean that you have to invest in Starbucks? Does it mean that this sudden spike is a prelude to more incredible profit margins? It does look too good to be true, right? What can you see from the historical data? One thing to remember is that whenever there has been a spike in the price value of Starbucks, there has been a decline soon.

One can never be certain if there will be a decline in the value of Starbucks. However, what you need to understand is that when something is too good to be true, it usually is.

Chapter 8: Position Entry and Exit Strategies

There are many traders who spend countless hours fine tuning their entry strategy. They reach a point where they are completely certain about their trade and are ready to make the next move. Eventually, they fail to create a successful trade and deplete their accounts soon all because they forgot to have a proper exit strategy.

Both your entry and exit strategies are important. One cannot be made without the other or else you are simply having half a plan.

Let's try to look at the basics of entering and exiting a position.

Reward and Risk Level

Since you aim to become a position trader, then you should ideally be looking (and you should be making a habit of this) at establishing a reward and risk targets. The first thing you need to do is to check out your chart and find out when the next resistance level might come into play based on the time period of your holding. This resistance level marks your reward target. We are going to look deeper into resistance and support targets. But for now, let's look at how you can establish your risk target. You simply have to choose the point that will prove that your risk has reached its limit. This point is the maximum risk that you can manage for the trade. Never try to keep your risk levels too low. You need to be realistic. Look at the funds you have and the amount you have spent on the trade. Try to evaluate your finances before deciding to choose the risk level.

Do Not Follow What Everyone Does

This is a common mistake among many traders. Whenever something happens, they begin to become part of a herd, as though being in a group gives them greater protection against the results of the trade. But that is not the case.

When a market starts correcting, you will see an increase the number of people selling the stocks. As the market dips further down, the number of people sales increases even more.

At this point, it does become a frightening prospect when you have to watch the prices of your stock dive further and further. What will happen to the stock? Are you going to face a huge loss on your investment?

Most people are afraid of loss and the eventual pain that it causes. When they see that the stock prices are going even lower, they sell because they do not want to lose any money. Experienced traders text in a more decisive manner. They have a strategy that they have implemented, and they usually stick to that strategy. They know the risk and reward points and how much they have invested. They have performed the analysis and are prepared for the sudden shifts in the market. In short, they are not playing the short-term game and not concerned with the results in the short-term.

These experienced traders know that simply reacting to one or a few buy and sell signals is not a wise idea. They know that their strategy is based on timing and it is for that reason that they will wait longer to see further changes in the prices of the stocks.

For more historical context to this phenomena I recommend the book *A Short History of Financial Euphoria* by legendary economist JK Galbraith.

Stop-Loss Strategy

Even though you decide that you are going to wait for the long-term results of your stock, it is also prudent to have a stop-loss strategy placed just in case.

A stop-loss strategy is simply an order that you place with your broker. It states that if the stock reaches a certain point, then the broker can buy or sell the stocks, depending on your strategy.

Let us take an example to highlight the above strategy. Let us assume that you have bought stocks of Microsoft Corporation (MSFT) at $40 per share. Immediately after buying the stock, you place a stop-loss order where you mention that if the stock price falls below $35, then the broker can initiate a sell order.

One of the advantages of placing a stop-loss order is that you do not have to keep a watch on the stock on a regular basis. You know that you are not going to suffer a major loss if things don't go your way. In fact, you are probably going to be safe (or safe as possible) with your investments.

Scaling Your Exit Strategies

When a new trade moves into a profit, then you can try to scale up your stop-loss order. This way, you are following the profit trend and at the same time, you are building confidence in trading. If you always keep a low stop-loss order and the price reaches that level, then you have missed an opportunity to make a profit. As you go along with the price increase, you are improving your chances of making a profit.

Stick to Your Plan

Make no mistake — your trading success depends on your ability to stick to your trading plan. Never deviate from that plan because every other decision might seem like the right thing to do. However, they are not the decisions that you had planned to take earlier. So, do not go down a path you are unfamiliar with. Besides, you are more concerned with the long-term effects of your trade. Do not let short-term changes affect the way you think about your trades and your plan.

Support and Resistance

Examine a chart. See the rise in the price of a stock. You will notice it rising until it reaches a certain point. After that, it begins to take a reverse course, falling. That point at which it pulls back is called the resistance.

In the same way, the lowest point that the price reaches before it begins to go back up is called the support.

But how do you trade with support and resistance levels?

Here are a few ways to use support and resistance in your trading.

Profit-Taking Strategies

Majors and Minors

In most cases, you might find that there are minor support levels on the charts. Only, these support levels are likely to be broken.

For example, let us assume that the price of the stock Apple Inc (AAPL) is dropping. It will reach a point after which it will bounce back. That point is called the minor support level. After a certain increase, the stock price will dip again. This time, it might pass your minor support levels.

When you use a minor support level, you gain more insights about the stock. If the price continues its downward trajectory, then you know that the stock's trend is intact. This will allow you to make some decisions. However, if the price bounces back up, then you know that a range could be developing. This range can give you the support and resistance levels of the stock price.

In case of the major level, we are looking at stocks that suddenly turn in the opposite direction after reaching a point. For example, if the price has been seeing an upward trend and suddenly starts going in a downward trend, then that point from which the price bounced is known as the major resistance level.

What's the difference between a minor level and a major level?

In a minor level, the price usually breaks through that level and continues onwards. In a major level, the price bounces and start going in the opposite direction.

Range Trading

Traders may sometimes choose to engage in range training, which takes place between the support and resistance levels. One of the things you have to remember is that the levels of support and resistance are not always perfect lines. Sometimes, they bounce off a particular area. It is also important to know that the support and resistance levels are not exact numbers. They are just levels that help you understand where you can find the support and resistance.

When the market is in a range, the traders are on the lookout for long entries were the prices bounce off a support level and short entries where the prices bounce off resistance levels.

Trendline Strategy

In this strategy, one uses the trendline as a support or resistance level. All you have to do is identify two or more highs in a downward trend of the price. This will allow you to create a support trendline. Similarly, if you can identify two or more lows in the upward trend of the price, then you will be able to draw a resistance trendline.

So, once you have these trendlines, then you should ideally be looking for entries along the trendlines. You should initiate a buy order along the support trendline and a sell order along the resistance trendline. This is because you are following certain trends and improving your odds of trading at a profit.

The False Breakout

The name "false breakout" is used appropriately and describes the situation perfectly. What it means is that the price of a stock was heading towards a breakout but failed to go beyond a particular level. This initiates a false breakout situation. False breakouts are an important indicator in trading because when a false breakout occurs, then it either means that the price is about to change direction or that there will be an occurrence of a trend.

A false breakout is also often described by the market as a form of deception. The reason is that the price looked like it was about to breakout but simply rebounded and headed in the opposite direction, making certain traders believe that it was going to breakout but instead, they get deceived by the price movement.

So, why do false breakouts happen?

Usually, it is the result of novice traders or those with "weak hands" (a market term for people who do not take any risks) enter the market at a point where they feel that they are safe to enter. This means that they enter the market when it is already headed towards a particular direction and then try to make a prediction about a breakout from a particular support or resistance level too quickly.

For professional traders, however, this is an opportunity. How can one trade during a false breakout?

Step 1: Look For a Swing Low

The first thing that you have to focus on is identifying the swing low, which is simply the low price movement of your stock. When you look at a chart, you will notice that the price usually moves in waves. When the price moves to certain low points within those waves and then bounces back up, then those points are termed as swing low.

The swing low lines are not necessarily the support line that we are looking for. This is because they often indicate a false breakout line.

However, swing lows can be used by traders who are holding a long position to find their stop-loss order.

What it tells us is that if there are multiple swing lows after a downward trend has been continuing for long, then that can indicate that a market bottom is about to take place. Traders can use this information to predict where they can set up their stop-loss or modify their strategy to meet the trend taking place.

Step 2: Below Swing Low

At this point, you should ideally wait for the stock to go below the swing low. In other words, you have to make sure that the price has gone below the false breakout line. Once the price reaches beyond this point, you can make your move.

At this point, traders can place a stop-loss order below the swing low in case there is a reversal in the price, and they would like to pull out fast. However, you are now waiting for the price to rise.

Step 3: Above Swing Low

In the next step, you are now waiting for the stock to go above the swing low. As it continues its upwards trend, you can stop-loss to go higher after each successful swing low. This way, you are moving up with the price. What you are doing in this scenario is that you are waiting for the stock to return to the upside.

When you have mastered the above steps, then you will have a clear idea of how you would like to buy and sell the stock. This will also help you manage your losses better and create an effective trading strategy.

Volatility Contraction

Trading with volatility contractions are an important way to trade stocks because you are using trends to work with your stocks.

Here is the truth of the market: it moves from a situation of high volatility to a situation of low volatility without any warning. In other words, the volatility is never constant. It always fluctuates based on market conditions and other factors.

When you are trading, you should usually enter into a period of low volatility. The reason is that the range on the charts get smaller as the volatility contracts.

Let's put it this way: When the market is at low-volatility, then you can easily predict the range and set up your stop-loss. In this manner, you have the advantage of setting up a tighter stop-loss. You can use this stop-loss on a big position size and still keep your risk as minimal as possible.

Setting Up Stop-Loss Properly

Nobody likes to lose money.

That is obvious, and it applies to everyone. The thing is, you cannot always avoid losing money in trading. However, what you can control is the amount of money that you lose. One of the biggest challenges that traders face is deciding where they would like to set up their stop loss order. Should they take more risks, or should they try and minimize the risk?

A stop-loss order, as we have seen earlier, is simply an order for your broker to sell your socks should the price of that stock falls below a particular point.

Let us assume that you have stocks worth $30 with you. You decide that your stop-loss point should be placed where the price drops by 10%. This means that you are going to place your stop-loss order at $30 minus the 10% criteria that you placed. This would be at $27.

Another strategy that you can apply is place a time period for your stop-loss. If your stock is not sold within a particular time period, they the broker will initiate a sale for you.

- The first thing that you are going to do is calculate the price of the stop-loss point. For this, you have to look at your chart and identify ranges of your stock over the course of therapist six months or more. Make sure you research the stock properly so that you have acclimated to its high points and low points.

- Now, calculate the median (or the midpoint line) on the chart.

- From that midpoint line, set up a stop-loss order anywhere between 4-7% from the median.

That is all there is to it. Make sure that you are well-versed with the trends of your chart before you begin to set up the stop-loss order.

When Do You Take Profits?

This is an important question that everyone asks themselves when they are trading. At what point should you consider taking in the profits? Do you have to take them when you see the first sign of an upward direction of the price of your stock? Should you wait longer?

Everyone likes to earn as much profit as possible. But the best way to improve your portfolio is to use the 20-25% rule. Here is how it works.

When you notice that the price is going in an upward trend, then allow it to go in that direction. When the price point has advanced by 20% or 25%, then you can initiate a sell order and take your profit. But why choose to stick to just 20% or 25% and not go higher? In many cases, the markets might hit corrections when the stock has advanced anywhere from 20% to 40%. When you apply the 20-25% rule, then you are allowing the price to go into the upward direction as much as possible before you pull out with a profit.

Chapter 9: Money Management

You are now used to fundamental and technical analysis. You can read the market and you know how to place your stop-loss orders. You are pretty much ready to take on the market and get your first profit!

However, there is one more important factor that you have to take into consideration before you begin to trade. You need to know how to manage your risk.

Most people do not ponder about how they should go about managing their risk. They think that as long as they are confident about their entry points, performed all the necessary research, and set up their stop-loss points, then they are good to go.

You need to know how to manage your risks or else everything you have learned until this point becomes rather moot.

Let us start off with the risk-and-reward assessment.

Risk/Reward Assessment

This assessment helps you understand just how much reward you are going to gain for the risk that you are placing in your trade.

Typically, the risk reward ratio is set at 2:1 so that you are compensated well for the risk that you have taken.

For instance, you are interested in the stock of a company called ARC. ARC is now trading at $30 from a previous trade price of $35. It has fallen by $5. You now have $600 with you to spend on this investment. After you have conducted your research and analysis, you believe that the stock price will go back up to $35 soon. You decide that you are going to buy 20 shares of the product. (With an investment of $600 and with $30 per share, you can buy a total of 20 shares).

Now that you have made the decision. You wait for the stock price to rise up. Let us assume that the stock price goes up to $35. Essentially, you have made a profit of $5 for each of the 20 shares you have with you. That is a total of $100.

You know that you are likely to get a profit of $100. Consider that you have put your stop-loss at $25. If you calculate that, then your risk is now $100. So, your risk is $100 while your reward is $100. This gives reward to risk ratio of 1:1. That is not ideal at all.

Now, let's say that we decide to change our risk amount. Rather than going for $25, we choose to go for $27.5 instead. Our risk now is only $2.5 per share or a total of $50. Our new reward to risk ratio is now 100/50. The new reward to risk ratio is 2:1. This seems more ideal to us at this point and we shall go ahead and take this reward to risk ratio.

Managing Trade Size

One of the most important decisions you will make in trading involves how much your trade size is going to be. Usually, you are going to use a percentage or dollar limit for each of the trades you are going to make.

Most traders choose not to risk more than 1% of their account on a single trade. Let's say that you have $10,000 in your account. With that amount, you are not going to risk more than $100 per trade. If you like, you can always go below that 1%, but you are going to decide never to go above the 1% mark.

Due to brokerage fees, this rule can be increased to 2% per trade if your total trading account is at $10,000 or less. But as a rule, you should never risk more than 2% of your account in a single trade.

This percentage rule that you set up will become your trade size.

Trading Journal

You can manage your performance by keeping a trade journal. Using this journal, you will be able to evaluate your past performance and then learn from your mistakes. When you want to succeed in the world of trading, then you need to have a lot of planning and understanding of the market. However, you may never know which of you plans had worked and which ones did not if you do not maintain a trade journal.

When you have a trading journal, you record each trade you have made along with all the details you can add about that trade. These details can then be reviewed in the future before you go on to start another trade. By doing so, you will not follow the same strategy if it had failed. On the other hand, if your previous strategy was a success, then you can continue to use it or find ways to modify it so it could produce better yields.

Additionally, when you have a trader journal, you become more and more analytical. You learn from each trade you make. This helps you remove the emotion out of the equation.

You begin to rely on raw data and information. You ignore the sudden impulses you receive when you are faced with a certain scenario. All you have to do is refer to your journal and see if you have faced the situation in the past.

Using Sample Trade Examples With Real Numbers

When you can learn from examples, then you may find yourself having more clarity when dealing with trades. However, do not choose to have an example that you cannot apply in real life. If you have real examples with real numbers, they are basically learning from a trade that has occurred in real life. This helps you find trades that are similar to yours or even learn some effective strategies from past trades.

When you use arbitrary numbers, then you are not sure if the strategy employed in that example will work or not since it hasn't actually happened.

Using real examples gives you confidence. In the world of trading confidence, it is the key to taking important decisions.

Consider the Golden Rule

Remember that even professional traders face losses. No one is immune to the effects of the stock market. Anybody can win or lose in trading.

What separates the novice from the experts, though, is the ability to handle the losses. When a new trader experiences loss, he or she then either starts paying too much attention to that loss or impulsively decides to make up for the loss by creating another mistake.

Expert traders, on the other hand, do not let their emotions get the better of them. They are focused. They analyze their losses and see what went wrong. Then, they ask themselves the following questions:

- Can the trade be salvaged?

- Should they return to the same trade?

- what have they done that led them to the loss?

- What can they do different?

- Was their strategy flawed? If so, is there something they should do to change their tactics?

They know that they can recover, if only they apply their logic to learn from their past losses.

Chapter 10: 7 Psychological Traps Every Trader Faces

Trading can be an intense scenario. The people who are not used to the psychological experiences of trading might not be prepared to face all the various psychological traps we might experience while trading. Let us look at some of these traps.

Trap #1: Confirmation Bias

We are always under the impression that we are people who are open to criticism and contradictory views. Unfortunately, psychology has a much different viewpoint than that. You see, we are usually biased. We look for information that supports our viewpoints and tend to ignore that information that contradicts our viewpoints.

This phenomenon is called "confirmation bias," and it is quite dangerous in the world of trading. We refuse to believe in the facts that seem to oppose the views that we have set up for ourselves. For example, whenever we suffer a loss, we might believe that there is a chance to bounce back. We become emotional after the loss that we fail to see the logical path: that we simply have to move on from that trade. However, our confirmation bias forces us to look for any bit of information that supports our theory that we are right and that the stock is capable of returning our investment.

In the world of trading, this is not always the case.

You need to be open to the idea that sometimes, the stocks have not worked out in your favor. You need to be able to accept the fact that you could be wrong about something.

Trap #2: Sunk-Cost Fallacy

Nobody likes to see all their hard work get flushed down the proverbial toilet. It is heartbreaking, disappointing, and sometimes a tough pill to swallow.

Defeats are part of the learning process. Through defeats, you understand what should be done and what should be avoided. They can guide you along the right part.

However, you can only learn from defeats if you allow them to teach you something. Many people delve into their defeats and refuse to acknowledge them.

This is what happens in a sunk-cost fallacy. In this fallacy, people continue a particular act, decision, or behavior because they have invested considerable money, effort, or time.

By doing so, people refuse to let go of such things, even if they are only going to cause more harm.

For example, let us imagine that Trader A has used a particular strategy for a trade. He or she has invested time and money to make sure that the trade reaps profitable results. Sadly, the trade ends up hitting a low, and Trade A realizes that the only thing he or she has gained is a losing trade. Rather than accepting the reality, Trader A continues to invest even more money and time into the trade.

Don't let that happen to you. Again, a loss is a loss.

Trap #3: Situational Blindness

Situational blindness is the distant cousin of confirmation bias. Sometimes, people may be choosing to willingly block out information from other sources, thinking that if they face those sources, then they might only receive bad news.

Whether you receive good or bad news, make sure that you are always getting your information right. Bad news is not the end of your trading life. However, ignoring bad news might just be.

Trap #4: Relativity Trap

Everyone has a unique psychological print. It's almost like a fingerprint, unique to each and every person. For this reason, not everyone might be looking at a trade using the same expectations, ideas, strategies, and information.

When you are entering a trade, therefore, make sure you keep your goals, available funds, and information at hand. Do not listen to people around you because they think they have a better idea for your trade.

It is alright to take valuable tips and information from veterans. In the end, you are the one who controls your trade.

Trap #5: Irrational Exuberance Trap

The past is not an indication of the future. Just because something has happened in the past does not mean that it will, with certainty, happen in the future. Believing that is putting yourself in a false sense of confidence. In fact, it can also be a situation of overconfidence, preventing you from looking at a trade with rational thought.

Trap #6: Superiority Trap

There is no limit to learning. Keep this in mind as you begin and continue trading. Always consider yourself as a student.

Often, you might come across traders who think that they know better than most people. In fact, just because they saw a YouTube video made by someone who has a "secret technique" or recently came across a book with insider tips, they feel that they know better than even veteran traders.

Do not let the feeling of superiority overwhelm you. Even if you think that you have learned everything there is to know about trading, keeping your focus on the information in front of you, listen to what other traders are saying with an open mind. Never forget as well that the more you learn, the more you earn.

Trap #7: Texas Sharpshooter Fallacy

Imagine a cowboy getting ready to shoot the side of a barn. His hands are poised on his revolvers. His face has a grim expression, like he's about the destroy the barn itself with his bullets. Quick as lightning, he whips out his revolvers and fires one shot after another into the side of the barn until his chambers are empty. He looks at the results and notices that the bullet holes are all over the wall. It looks like he is not a good shot after all, but what he does next is quite perplexing.

He walks up to the wall, takes out a chalk, draws a circle around a random cluster of bullet holes and then exclaims, "See? I have hit bullseye!"

He hadn't actually hit bullseye. He created a bullseye himself. He created order around a random distribution of bullet holes.

As humans, we do not like to feel that things are arbitrary. We love to place order on chaos. Unfortunately, this might pose a problem to us because we start creating connections between a random assortment of facts, even when no such connections exist. When you are trading and you notice a collection of information, do not attempt to draw conclusions by yourself. Do not make connections when there are not. Just like the bullet holes, do not group together random information and think that you may have found a valuable secret.

Always follow the facts. If you spot something, use your due diligence to find out more about it.

Never assume anything. It is fun to watch characters in movies look really smart by finding a pattern in a cluster of information. But that is not how real life works. Even veterans do not try to find patterns. They simply follow the information and see where it leads them.

Conclusion

Position trading is a long-term strategy.

That is something you have to keep in mind before you enter into position trading. You see, many people forget the fact that they are going to have to wait for months to see the progress their trade makes. They get so caught up in the small details or the short-term changes of their stock. This compels them to make some rather hasty decisions.

The main reason for choosing position trading is that it is supposed to add less stress into your life. What's the point of worrying about the small details and increasing your stress levels? Sure, you do have to monitor your trades every day, but you are not concerned about all the changes that happen every day.

Leave the daily strategy for the day traders.

Remember that even though position trading is a long-term strategy, it is is much safer than other forms of trading. In most trading forms, you are looking at changes that happen every single day. If you miss out on one single piece of information or trend change, then you are going to miss out on an opportunity to make profits.

The most important factor for you to remember is that you need to learn everything you can from this book so you can strengthen your foundation. By going through the basics, you are creating an understanding of the market. As you deal with the market, you build upon the foundation you have laid down, getting better with every trade that you make.

One of the biggest advantages is that you can get involved with position trading while having a full-time job as well. This is ideal for people who do not want to give up on their career for trading. They simply have to spend 30 minutes every day to look through your stock and see if you need to make any small adjustments.

Always be prepared before any trade. Understand your trade size. Check your stop-loss and other strategies. It is only when you are sure of everything that you should decide to enter into a trade.

Do not let your emotions overwhelm you. Keep your mind focused on the information you have, not on the emotions you feel.

Happy trading!

Swing Trading for Beginners

7 Golden Rules for Making a Full-Time Income Online with Routines, Proven Strategies and Risk Management + Guides for Trading Cryptocurrency & Forex

Introduction

If you have the intent and the capital to start operating in the stock market, the only other thing you need is a strategy. Stock trading strategies are usually a tried and tested way of transacting that gives you the confidence you need to engage profitably in the stock market. One of the most effective strategies of operating in the stock market is swing trading. With swing trading, you only take up a stock position when there is an anticipated upswing in the price of a stock.

Swing trading requires active participation to identify impending changes in the price of a stock and act on them. And even though you don't have to watch every tiny dip and surge in the price, the background research needed for every transaction and volume of trades you will need to do to make it a profitable engagement might prove distracting. As such, swing trading is an activity you probably want to do as a full-time career. The good thing is that it is extremely easy to make good money off it. The prices of stocks are always changing; it is the one thing we can always count on. In a world full of uncertainty, change is the only constant.

The stock market is no different. In fact, it could be the one sector of the economy that best reflects the realities of change. Stock prices are always changing; rising in price in response to rising demand and dropping due to investor disinterest or negative news. Swing trading takes advantage of these fluctuations, buying stocks at their lowest price levels and selling at the peak for maximum profit-making.

The internet has been one of the greatest agents of change in the world and the stock market has been no different. It has witnessed massive change ever since electronic trading became a reality. You see, before the advent of electronic communication, all transactions in the stock market had to be done in these quaint houses called the stock exchanges. Traders would agree on new stock prices by engaging in yelling matches, the news was passed through newspapers and word of mouth, and every trade was done on paper, leaving a large 'paper trail.'

Today, the stock exchange is an abstract idea that references the activity of exchanging stock ownership rather than the place where the activity takes place. With your mobile device, you can access each and every stock exchange in the world and buy or sell stocks of any company from anywhere with the mere press of a button. News aggregation websites bring you the news before they break in the mainstream media. In fact, the only thing you need to start a career in stock trading today is an internet connection and some money to buy shares with!

But after all is said and done, stock trading is a huge gamble. You can never be assured on actually making money from your stock position, which makes it even more important to devise a fool-proof strategy. And swing trading may sound a little overwhelming, but it doesn't have to be! You can simply learn 2 or 3 profitable trading strategies and execute them in 90% of scenarios. The better you get at executing your strategies, the more profitable a trader you will become.

See, I was once just like you; clueless, unsure, and inexperienced. My journey began when I was 18, my grandfather gave me $500 to invest in the stock market. Ironically, he would lose over 90% of his holdings in the 2008 crash a few months later. I later learned later that he had nearly all his wealth concentrated in just a handful of bank and telecom stocks.

I took that $500 and bought 12 shares of McDonald's.

My teenage reasoning at the time was that I'd never seen an empty McDonald's restaurant. I was so naïve I didn't even appreciate the real estate element of McDonald's business model. However, my rather amateurish logic paid off and I still have those 11 shares (and many more) today. They have since multiplied by around 450%. That was also the starting point for my stock ownership and trading career.

You can have that life too. A good salary from a job where you are your own boss, set your own hours, have all the free time you want to vacation, and work remotely from whatever location you want. All this is achievable if you are willing to put in the time and learn the ropes. And the good news is that you can achieve it all with a simple-to-use array of mobile applications and computer software. And even though you will read a lot about the different strategies of trading, ultimately, you will end up with the one best suited to your trading goals.

Veterans of stock trading attest to this fact. Brian Pezin, the founder of Bear and Bull Traders (bearandbulltraders.com) has used the same 3 strategies for all his trades and he has made a fortune. He now uses his experience to help other traders to achieve their potential making money in the stock market.

This book familiarizes you with all the information you need to establish a successful stock trading career. It equips you with the insights on where to start, what to expect from swing trading, and how to come up with your own unique strategy based on your personal trading goals. And even though we will teach you the methods through which you can start making money from trading, we cannot promise that you will make money by applying these strategies. It is crucial that you acknowledge from the word go that sometimes things don't go your way. But even when this happens, you should find the motivation to carry on until you find a strategy that works for you. Whatever mistakes you make along the way will only make the journey that much more fulfilling.

You will also learn what makes swing trading different from other common methods of stock market operation, mainly stock trading and investing. Straddling the line between the speculative nature of day trading and the long-term positioning of investing, swing trading is more of an opportunistic operation that takes advantage of price changes to make money.

A full description of the different instruments that can be swung is also given. These include stocks, ETFs, FOREX, and cryptocurrency. Each one of these instruments requires a unique strategy to make money from it. By understanding how they all operate, you will have a better chance to identify the best time to enter a trade and the right time to exit, which is essentially the best way to establish a steady income stream for yourself.

This is not a 'get rich quick' book. Any book or system that promises you instant returns or guaranteed profit-making is lying to you. Anything worth doing takes time to learn and that is very true for this particular strategy. Before learning the ropes, you might stumble and make false moves. Heck, you will probably lose some money. But if you keep at it and learn from all your mistakes, then I guarantee that you will soon be making more money than you know what to do with it.

And because this book will also teach you how to manage your money, you will be able to handle this extra income in a productive manner. The training you will receive on money management will also come in handy when you will be learning to deal with the risk that is inherent in the stock market.

Thousands of average Americans have made a fortune in the stock market. With swing trading, your money can work for you and any activity you do fits perfectly into your current lifestyle. By learning to play the market, you can have enough money to live that idyllic life you have always wanted. All the money and all the time (well, maybe not ALL, but a whole lot of it) to have as much fun as you desire. With proper money management, you only need to win in 55% of your trades to be profitable. If you follow this guidebook and persevere through any initial hiccups, you will be right on your way to making some serious money. Let's get on with it now, shall we?

Chapter 1: How Swing Trading Works

Anyone who has observed the price chart for any financial asset will attest to the fact that prices change in an undulating style. While day traders worship at the feet of price fluctuation and investors snub any sort of short-term price fluctuations, they present a fertile ground for a different kind of short-term investor to benefit- the swing trader. With swing trading, investors take up a position in an asset for just long enough to give it time to reach the highest level of that particular price move. The general timeframe for swing trading is usually a few weeks to several months, which allows you to capture a huge chunk of profits from an ascending asset.

You can profit from a swing position with stocks, exchange-traded funds, cryptocurrency, Forex, and options among other financial assets. Basically, any asset that has high price volatility has the potential to be swing traded. In the stock market, swing trading follows the same fundamental principles of day trading, but with higher exposure to market elements because the longer time span of swing trading encompasses weekends and after-hours trading activity. Subsequently, the money you will make in a swing trade will be significantly higher.

Investing and trading exist at opposite ends of stock market operation. One requires years upon years of waiting while the other mostly ignores market factors that cause stock prices to rise and fall.

Swing Trading Vs. Investing

Most financial advisors recommend investing over trading for the simple reason that investing has more assured returns. With up to 20 years in which to manipulate your portfolio, you can correct any mistakes you make in the first years and still turn up a good reward in the end. But what if you don't have all that time? Swing trading gives a perfect alternative to investing that is not day trading, which is considered too risky and more like betting than anything else.

Swing trading differs from investing in one main area; swing traders are more opportunistic than investors. While an investor retains ownership of stock for years before liquidating and taking profits, the swing trader is more of the cunning fox who comes in just before there is a bump in the stock price and liquidates as soon as they have made their targeted profit in that particular transaction. The upside to this strategy is that you don't have to wait years, watching anxiously as the stock price rises and plunges. The rises and plunges become your calling card- a never-ending source of money for you.

And market volatility? That will become your best friend! The very thing that for investors is a fearsome enemy, doubles up as an enabler for swing traders. In fact, stock market volatility is the only reason why it is possible to swing trade. Those rises and drops bring with them a cash windfall that only the most adroit can cash in on. In the following twelve chapters, you will learn how to become one of these clever people.

You see, people like Warren Buffett can afford to keep billions upon billions of dollars in the stock market, taking up lasting positions and profiting on dividends and dividend reinvestment plans to secure for themselves an even bigger profit. Any person saving up for retirement in over twenty years, someone with a full-time job and the desire to retire comfortably when the time comes, can also afford to keep their money tied up for decades. By following a determinedly conservative investment strategy and rarely transacting directly in the stock market, people with other sources of income, no current need for their money, and no intention to enjoy their handiwork until they are old and graying follow the investment route.

Swing trading is for the other kind of gentleman; the one who wants to make their money and make it now; the one who does not want to wait until they are 50 to start living right. With a little more effort, the swing trader engages in tens or hundreds of transactions and creates a more substantial income for themselves. And the good news is that you don't need to do it full time. With robo-advisors, you can simply give buy and sell commands to your virtual assistant on a select number of stocks. Whenever the price is right, your VA will automatically buy or sell a pre-arranged number of stocks. Talk about passive income!

But here is the most interesting interplay between the world of investing (especially large capital investors like Warren Buffett and institutional investors) and that of swing trading. When these parties make a move in the stock market, the stock market responds in a huge way. For example, if Berkshire Hathaway plans to buy 7% of a small cap company today, they would have to keep taking up all the stocks that come into the market until they reach the desired level. This will take anywhere between a few weeks and a few months, during which time the stock price is almost assuredly going to peak steadily. Any time an acquisition or merger or big business move entails a stock swap, the stock price usually climbs as investors capitalize.

For a swing trader, these sorts of moves make for fertile ground in their quest for profit-making. As the big players make their big money moves, taking up a stock position when the stock price is still low means that you will be likely to see a sharp upward movement in the short term. And while big money players don't make their moves very often, whenever a huge transaction goes down, swing traders who are well-positioned stand to reap the rewards. The trick, therefore, is to learn how to identify the triggers before they become glaringly apparent to the whole market.

In essence, here are the reasons why you may choose to swing-trade rather than invest. At number one is to avoid anxiety. If you are the kind of person who can't stand the upward and downward swing of the stock price chart, then the shorter holding period of stock trading is perfect for you. Since you only hold a stock for one upward swing before divesting, there will be few (if any at all) price fluctuations before you hit your selling level.

Another reason to swing trade rather than invest is that it is more thrilling. With long-term investing, your profits are made over a long time and you will hardly ever have those make or break moments when you are practically at the edge of your seat in anticipation. With swing trading, you have to stay sharp and focused because if you miss your shot, you have no time to recover. The margins for stop-loss selling are very low with swing trading because swing traders can't stand the drops in price that investors consider to be perfectly safe.

Swing Trading Vs. Day Trading

Traders make the stock market go round. They define, by and large, the price at which a stock trades at by their buying and selling activity. When traders panic and divest the shares of a particular company in a short time, they bring the price to rock-bottom level. In the same vein, enthusiasm about a particular stock sends it skyrocketing. In the institution of stock trading, we have the day trader, an investor who buys and sells a block of a company's stocks in the course of a trading day. A swing trader differs from the day trader in that he holds his position for a short period of time, which is normally more than a day but less than a month. Swing traders usually buy in anticipation of an increase in the stock price. In essence, it is an improvement on day trading that reduces risk and increases gains. Swing trading is better than day trading in the instances described below.

Avoiding instant stop-loss plummets: swing trading with the right strategies means that you are wise enough to avoid those instances of bad luck where you buy a stock and it plummets right through your stop-loss price (yes, it happens, and quite often at that too).

Day trading is the riskiest of all stock market operations. The chances that a stock will suddenly plunge are very high. And even scarier is the fact that a single transaction can lead to the plunge that cheats you of any anticipated gains. The extended holding time for swing trading insulates from the extreme sensitivity to price that plagues day trading.

Another reason why swing trading trumps day trading is the profit margins. With day trading, your profit margins are extremely low. So low in fact, that some transactions are done at the earliest point when selling will leave the trader with some money after paying taxes and commission fees. Swing trading capitalizes on huge price surges brought about by external factors to make large profits in a few short weeks. With proper intelligence and the ability to predict future prices, you can be making as much profit in one month as an investor makes in two years.

And if you think that swing trading is too time-consuming, then wait until you learn all about the time commitment demanded by day trading. With such low margins of profit for every trade, the only way to make some money is to engage in as many transactions as possible- make money on volume trading. Day traders start hunting for a new position to take immediately after exiting the current one. With swing trading, you will have a few days or weeks to look for new positions after exiting your current one. The time commitment you need to swing trade is the same as that which it takes to read two or three chapters in a book or the news. With the strategies discussed in the coming chapters of this book, you can cut down even further on this time with some specialized tools.

But when considering day trading versus swing trading, the greatest difference comes in at the capital commitment required for either one of them. With day trading, you are legally required to keep at least $25,000 in your brokerage account. No such requirement is placed on swing trading. The money you keep in your account is entirely up to you.

Retail Vs. Institutional Traders

Retail traders explain even further how swing traders profit from moves made by large investors like Warren Buffett and other institutional investors. When these large buyers/sellers transact, they put up a sell or buy order for a share of their total desired shares and trade over a few days until they reach their desired level. These institutional investors, when they engage in trading rather than investing, are called institutional traders (of course) and operate on behalf of larger groups like mutual funds, insurance companies, exchange traded funds, among others.

Institutional traders sometimes receive preferential treatment on the bidding and setting of prices for a transaction. These advantages have been reduced by the advent of online stock transactions because they now have the same platforms to trade as individual (retail) traders. However, the impact of institutional traders is still markedly greater than that of individual traders. With a larger volume of stocks to divest or take up, institutional traders invariably cause a glut or shortage of stocks in the market, triggering the law of supply and demand on a particular stock.

Retail traders are the unchallenged majority in the stock market. Their dominance insofar as setting prices goes is only limited by their plurality. Because each person holds but a few shares, their activity has little impact on the rest of the market. Only through herd mentality can retail traders have a remarkable effect on the rest of the market.

Open Hours Vs. Aftermarket Trading

You may have heard analysts mention the phrase "after-hours trading." Sometimes the price of a stock goes up in after-hours trading because some positive news broke out. In some cases, the price plummets because some negative news broke out. Activity in the stock market that takes place outside the 9:30 am to 4:00 pm timeslot is collectively referred to as after-hours trading.

But more specifically, the morning hours before the markets open are referred to as the pre-market session. Depending on the investor confidence (or lack thereof) about a stock, the pre-market trading session could set up a stock for massive trading and price rise or deflate it and bring the price down. In the evening hours, after-hours trading allows interested traders to continue transacting. The activity here often dissipates by the next morning, so prices traded during after-hours activity are not usually assured to last till the next day's trading session.

When considering aftermarket trading, you need to understand a few things about the whole concept. First off, not all brokerage firms allow for aftermarket trading and for those that do, the window varies. For example, TD Ameritrade opens its after-hours trading session 15 minutes after the close of the trading day and keeps it open all the way to 8:00 pm (the end of after-hours trading for most brokerage firms) while Wells Fargo opens much earlier at 4:05 pm and closes much earlier as well at 5:00 pm.

Another thing to consider is the commission fees charged. Most brokerage firms like E-Trade, charge more for aftermarket trading. More significantly, not all assets can be traded in aftermarket trading. And more limiting terms are placed on those that can actually be moved aftermarket. For example, stop orders, all-or-none orders, mutual funds, bonds, and options cannot be made outside of the market hours.

Finally, with fewer people engaging in aftermarket trading, you will have to deal with lower liquidity issues, leading to a huge bid-ask spread. The low liquidity comes with another caveat- high volatility. This is especially true when market-shaking news comes out because investors rush to give sell or buy orders as soon as possible.

With the right swing trading techniques, your money can work for you without disrupting your current lifestyle. And if you have an ideal lifestyle that you are working towards, swing trading can fit perfectly into it. Just be sure not to build your lifestyle around swing trading and instead build your swing trading business around your lifestyle, current or desired.

And by learning to play the market, you can have enough money to live that idyllic life you have always wanted. All the money and all the time (well, maybe not ALL, but a whole lot of it) to have as much fun as you desire.

Chapter 2: Best Trading Software

To be a successful swing trader, you are going to need the right tools. Apart from the trading software that every Tom, Dick, and Harry uses, it is important that you bolster your operation with scanning software to keep you updated with the most recent news in the stock market. After all, what is swing trading if not the art and science of identifying short-term trends and positioning yourself to benefit?

Trading software gives you a way into the stock market, allowing you to bid and offer shares to the rest of the stock-buying populace. But, of course, all trading software is not equal. Different brokerage firms offer their services on different platforms, including desktop applications, browser-based portals, mobile apps and websites, and the good old voice commands where you simply call your transaction in. This last function can be handy especially when your internet is not all that reliable.

Trade execution also differs from platform to platform and from service to service. Some take a few minutes to refresh, meaning that the prices you see are usually a few minutes old, while others bring you real-time prices as they appear in the price chart at NASDAQ, NYSE, or whatever other stock markets your broker is affiliated to.

Now, I may have hinted at this before, but am just going to come out and say it. Swing trading is entirely a matter of intelligence gathering. Just like kickass CIA agents scour the underworld to keep enforcement agencies informed about the goings on in the underworld, so should every kickass swing trader keep tabs on the stock market. If a development happens with some terrorist cell without the CIA knowing, lives could be at risk. If a development happens with some stock and you as a swing trader don't know about it, your livelihood will definitely be at risk.

Scanning software enables you to stay abreast of developments in the stock market. And with really good scanners, you can receive the inside scoop before it reaches the market, enabling you to take a profit-making position when prices are still low.

Best Online Brokers

Online brokers have come to revolutionize the way the stock market operates. No longer do traders need to congregate in noisy trading floors and yell orders over each other. The piles of paperwork that traders filled out to complete a trade have been replaced by neat electronic tools that allow remote transactions at the touch of a button. So, whether you are off vacationing in Tahiti or lounging on your couch at home, online brokers got you covered. But just which online brokers are leaders of the pack?

According to the good people at Investopedia (which is a great source of information for the financial markets), the five best brokers of 2019 are; Fidelity Investments, Interactive Brokers, Charles Schwab, TradeStation, and TD Ameritrade in that order. As an investment-centric broker, Charles Schwab falls out of our listing for the best online brokers, to be replaced by E-Trade and Ally, which are pretty amazing too. In the course of this chapter, we will analyze each of these brokers and run a comparison for some.

Let's start with **Fidelity Investments**. Established in 1946 as a cash management and research company, Fidelity has grown to become one of the largest stockbrokers not just in America, but in the world. The company had revenues of over \$18 billion as of 2017 and assets worth more than \$2 trillion (yes, trillion) under their management. Fidelity Investment's online brokerage services are some of the best in the country because they are supported by a long history of operations and over 50,000 employees in more than 140 locations around the country. And even though the online brokerage service is totally autonomous, it is always good to know that you can upgrade to a more supported account where you can consult with investment specialists in any of the company's offices closest to you.

Fidelity offers a dizzying range of financial assets for you to choose from, ranging from stocks, mutual funds, ETFs, 401k plans, index funds, cryptocurrency, securities, and REITs among others. Another great thing with Fidelity Investments is that it has complete banking capabilities so you can withdraw straight from your brokerage account to a drawing account without moving money between banks.

You will get a wide variety of platforms to choose from with Fidelity Investments, but each one has been calibrated to offer you the best trade executions possible. The Active TraderPro is especially outstanding as a trading tool.

Interactive Brokers is another outstanding online stockbroker. It has the largest number of internationally traded assets and tools for round-the-clock trading. In fact, with 120 markets, 31 countries, and 23 currencies represented, Interactive Brokers sure earned the award for Best International Trading. With it, it is possible to buy and sell futures, options, and equities anywhere in the world at any time of the day- a quality that makes it especially favorable for those who find the allure of trading in odd hours irresistible.

Interactive also has an amazing robo advisory service. This means that with a few simple settings, you can activate your stocks for automatic selling when the market reaches your target price at any time of the day. This comes in especially handy if you have to juggle swing trading and another job or activity. The icing on the cake that is Interactive Brokers is that their fees are the lowest of any brokerage firms of its caliber. In fact, Interactive Brokers has the lowest fees of all brokers discussed in this section. Considering that it also ranks highly on other metrics, this broker is an especially good choice for the price conscious swing trader. The only underside to an otherwise excellent option is that unlike brokers like Fidelity and Ally, it does not have banking facilities attached.

TradeStation is the fourth best online broker in our list. It is highly focused on outstanding customer care, faultless trade execution, and the best market data of any online broker on this list. This range of products makes TradeStation an excellent choice for volume traders, a category that any swing trader falls into. Moreover, you can devise a custom trading system using the tools offered in the platform, including statistical modeling of strategies and technical analysis.

Another outstanding online broker is **E-Trade**, an exclusively internet based brokerage firm that was started in 1982 to offer stock traders an online platform to buy and sell stocks. E-Trade's online platform is one of the oldest in the stock market today, offered since the days of America Online. With the trading platforms upgraded over decades of use, E-Trade boasts one of the best trading platforms in the market. The price charts available on the platform are usually in real time, which makes it even more suitable when there is only a small window of opportunity to make money before prices plummet.

TD Ameritrade is one of the most popular brokers available for you as a swing trader.

It has probably the largest number of users (over 10 million) and facilitates more transactions on a given day than any other broker (over 900,000). Not only does TD Ameritrade offer great price comparison tools, it also allows you to do your analysis right in the platform before making a transaction.

Finally, we have Ally Invest, a division of Ally Bank that gives you some of the best prices, including some free trades when you deposit $10,000 or more. In fact, Ally offers more competitive prices than ETrade and TD Ameritrade, even though it is still higher than Interactive Brokers. The opening balance of $1 makes Ally especially great for beginners, allowing you to build up your investment over time with deposits and plowed-back profits.

Comparison

Each of the brokers analyzed above have their upsides and downsides, making every one of them suited to different types of traders. For example, with its rock-bottom commission fees, Interactive Brokers is the best for margin-conscious traders who would like to keep as much of their profits as they can. Ally is perfect for investors who have just a little cash to start trading with. With competitively priced fees, Ally also enables you to build up your account holding over time by charging very little of your trades in fees.

With E-Trade, you get an averagely priced broker, but one whose platforms are excellently tuned for stock trading, with real-time prices and first-rate trade execution. On the other hand, TD Ameritrade is very committed to providing its users with the best materials to learn stock trading. Combine that with its top-of-the-range price analysis and trade execution tools and you have a very competitive broker too.

Then we have the brokers that have a banking service linked, which increases the suitability for brokers like Ally and Fidelity. These brokers provide you with greater convenience while topping up your account with money for trades and when you need to withdraw from your brokerage account into a drawing account.

In the end, your choice for a brokerage firm depends simply on what you prioritize between discounted commission and fees, the least minimum opening balance, ease of trade execution, and ease of access for your money.

Full-Service Vs. Discount Brokers

The choice between a full-service and a discount broker is one that cannot be made very lightly. It is a matter of choosing between quality services and cost-effectiveness. full-service and discount brokers differ on commission and fees, research and education tools, minimum opening balances, and the range of financial assets offered.

A full-service broker does not just make it possible for you to buy and sell stocks. They offer services like financial advice, portfolio management, and for those who prefer, a full-service broker can even make decisions on what assets to buy on your behalf. A full-service broker will do all the due diligence research for you, saving up hours you would otherwise spend learning various stock market operations. Subsequently, full-service brokers charge premium fees, sometimes going up to twenty times the cost of discount brokers. Because of the personal attention the broker will have to give to every account, the minimum opening balances and account minimums are fittingly huge, with some requiring at least $100,000 to start.

Discount traders are so called because they charge discount prices for their services. Because the broker only facilitates but does not execute buy and sell orders, you get to pay only a tiny fraction of what you would have paid with a full-service broker. And even though they don't give you any financial advice, discount traders will avail a range of materials to teach you how to go about making investing decisions. Another feature of discount brokers is that they have very low or non-existent minimum balances. The only minimum balances you will need to maintain in your account are those that are legally required, like the $25,000 that is needed for a day-trading brokerage account to remain operational.

Full-service brokerage accounts are suited for investing and trading respectively. An investor who wants to access their money in twenty years and has $1 million to invest can benefit from the human touch of full-service brokers as well as their investment prerogative to make investments on behalf of their clients. And even though every transaction attracts a hefty commission fee, the fact that only a few of them will be completed every year means that it will not become a huge issue.

Discount brokers are designed almost specifically for trading. The low commission fee is very suitable for volume trades; otherwise, it becomes too expensive to run your trading operation. Even with the limited education materials, you can still bolster your knowledge on the stock market and establish a profitable operation. As long as you keep an eye out for the minimum balances, annual subscription fees, and opening balances, there is no reason why your discount broker shouldn't be an absolutely perfect fit for your swing trading needs.

Stock Scanning Resources

When the only chance you have of making a profit from a trade is a price change that happens within minutes or a few hours, then you are definitely going to need a stock scanner. A stock scanner helps you achieve the perfect execution of trades, taking advantage of tight spreads to avoid a costly slip that could deny you a great profit. The last thing you want to do is make a mistake like buying an asset and wind up selling at the lowest point (stop loss) after you missed out on the price surge that you expected and that made you buy the stock in the first place. Timing is everything in the highly volatile stock trading environment.

Identifying stocks that are likely to experience a surge in the coming days is another skill that every stock trader could do very well to have. With artificial intelligence algorithms, you can discover these stocks and identify the best strategy to trade in them, determine the most effective position size for the transaction, and even automate the selling order at a particular price. While stock scanners give real-time data on stocks to allow you to make that snap buy or sell order, screeners use slightly delayed data, but they give you a fantastic opportunity to peruse capital markets using technical criteria like Moving Average Cross, Candlestick Patterns and fundamental standards like Industry Dividends and Market Cap. Stock screeners help you identify potentially profitable stocks and possibly maintain a catalog of the prospective future swing positions you might take.

And while you can possibly make do without a stock screener (there are numerous other ways to identify stocks with the potential for profit-making), a stock scanner is absolutely indispensable. The power to identify trading opportunities as they become available so as to position yourself to profit is one that you simply cannot do without. And as we saw above, the cost of missing trading opportunities could be absolutely fatal for a swing trader. Luckily, most stock scanners come with an embedded screener, which negates the need for you to find one of your own. Some of the best stock scanners in the market right now include Chartmill and Finviz.

Chartmill

Chartmill is one of the best paid-service stock scanning tools in the market. Available as a web-based platform as well as a mobile app, it comes with a sophisticated array of charting, analysis, and deep scanning tools. The charts are well-updated, with a choice between lines, bars, and candlesticks as well as different time frames ranging from monthly, weekly, and of course daily. Using various scanning metrics offered in the platform, you can identify those needle-in-the-haystack stocks quite easily with Chartmill. However, keep an eye out on your credit, because it might be depleted while you pull charts and scan away.

And like any good stock screener, Chartmill allows you to create a watch list. You can customize your lists by sector, expected swing rate, and price patterns. And to build on these capabilities, the application also gives you the opportunity to generate alerts and pop-up notifications when the market attains certain conditions or a particular price is reached. You also get to choose between email and intra-application notifications.

Finviz

Finviz prides itself in its ability to provide users with the perfect balance between researching and the actual trading activities. With the stakes being as high as they are for you in the stock market, it is possible that you get so carried away with researching that you don't get the time to factor in the big-picture objective of investing in the stock market in the first place- making money. With a powerful set of fundamental and technical research tools, Finviz aims to offer you the best financial analysis, research, and visualization, accessible at the touch of a button and easily digestible to negate the need for you to spend hours on it.

With a freemium price model, Finviz free gives you screening, charts, and quotes, but you will have to contend with adverts while you do your thing. On the other hand, paying subscribers get an ad-free trading experience, data that is refreshed in real time, intraday charts, alerts, and fundamental charts. Apart from these features, Finviz also offers information like news releases on a featured stock's earnings, major news, and insider trading clues. The information is actually rather overwhelming, but if you can learn to compartmentalize and look beyond the fluff to identify the critical information, Finviz will become absolutely indispensable. In fact, Finviz is considered by many analysts to be the most versatile, flexible, and user-friendly screener in the market today. With just a few clicks, Finviz enables you to identify stocks that fit your criteria based on price, patterns, average volume, float short, and outstanding shares among other measures. In essence, you get total control over the scanning process, with a customization function that allows you to make future scans using tried and tested metrics.

And just like any good scanner, Finviz also has a news service that offers headline news from various financial news services like MarketWatch, Wall Street Journal, Bloomberg, NBC, CNN, and PR Newswire. Other news is streamed from blogs like Seeking Alpha, Mish Talk, Vantage Point Trading, Zero Hedge, and others. With this large collection of news sources, you can search for the most current information about a company and get a diverse list of articles to help you along.

News Sources

Early in the morning of June 8, 2016, Tesla Inc. CEO Elon Musk sent the price of two stocks trending in different directions after he announced (via tweeter) that Tesla would be stocking with Panasonic in the processing of Model 3 fuel cells. The tweet followed in the wake of widespread speculation that the company was planning to switch to Samsung as a strategic partner in the same. When the stock markets opened a few hours later, $580 million was quickly wiped from Samsung's market cap while Panasonic's rose by $800 million. In the afternoon hours of February 8, 2017, newly inaugurated President of the United States Donald Trump sent a tweet attacking Nordstrom for dropping his daughter's clothing line. Within minutes of the tweet being sent (and being featured in feverish news broadcasts by all the main cable news services) $86 million had been wiped off Nordstrom's market as investors rushed to sell it off. And while the resistance movement managed to turn the tide and send the price into an upward trend, ending the day with a 4% rise.

These two scenarios are just a few of the hundreds, possibly thousands, of scenarios when events outside the stock market caused a stock to respond in a certain way within a very short time. They serve as a perfect indication of the crucial role that real-time news has for a swing trader. Imagine receiving the news that Panasonic had just been confirmed to be the uncontested partner in a billion-dollar endeavor with one of the most eligible automotive companies in the world. The obvious expectation is that investor confidence would go up and cause the price to rise substantially. By taking up a position at the earliest opportunity, you would get the perfect opportunity to make a profit in just a few hours.

Clearly, breaking news about a company has a huge impact on the price of its stock. The news does indeed move markets. Therefore, adding a news aggregation tool to your portfolio of trading resources will help to keep you as well-informed as possible and actually give you insider-like information about impending price changes. For this very noble purpose, you will need the best breaking financial news service in the market. And none can raise a candle to Scoop Markets.

Scoop Markets

Scoop Markets is a very simple tool with a very simple purpose; it informs you any time significant developments takes place, but before the news makes it to the mainstream media. Some of the most outstanding predictions made by Scoop Markets include an event during which a strategic partnership between IoT cryptocurrency firm Waltonchain and Alibaba on 5th March 2018 caused a 40% surge in the former's stock price. Scoop Markets' algorithms recognized the impending partnership a full 34 hours before the two companies announced it.

Scoop Markets predicts other financial assets apart from stocks. For example, on 13th July 2018, it predicted an impending price bump in the token price of Crypto after the company launched an iOS wallet. A 33% price upsurge in 3 hours followed the news alert.

So how does Scoop Markets do it? The firm's algorithms scan through thousands of tweets every second, trying to identify breaking news before it happens. With the largest pool of technical analysis tools of any news analysis service, Scoop Markets performs in-depth diagnostics before sending alerts and trading signals. The wise swing trader takes these alerts and acts on them.

Chapter 3: Different Financial Instruments You Can Trade

It is common knowledge that stocks are not the only financial assets you can trade in the stock market. There are numerous other assets that are equally liquid and profitable. But for the swing trader, only financial assets that experience steep upswings in price from time to time are eligible to be put on the watch list. And the watch list is to the swing trader what the investment portfolio is to the investor- indispensable. Apart from stocks, some of the most swing tradable financial assets include Exchange Traded Funds (ETFs), Cryptocurrency, Forex, and options. In the sections below, we define each one of them and explain how they can be swing traded.

Stocks

Stocks are the most commonly swing traded financial assets. After the price is set during the IPO, the price of a stock corresponds with the investors' confidence in the future financial prospects of the mother company. So, whenever positive news is released, the stock price rises. And any time a negative news item comes out, you can expect the price to go down.

The most obvious way to swing trade stocks is to identify companies that are about to release some very positive, confidence-boosting news. Generally speaking, the most effective strategies to swing stocks are when you recognize a future surge in price, which is most often caused by positive news. For example, with a pharmaceutical or consumer electronics company, prior to a new product that is expected to perform well, you can buy the stock at very low prices and, just a few weeks or months later, sell them at a higher price and make a killing. Other predictors of future price hikes include strategic partnerships with a prominent company, a merger, an announcement for a huge dividend payout (which indicates a great financial situation at the company), or even a company that has not been doing too well hiring a new rock star CEO.

ETFs

Exchange Traded Funds track a collective of financial assets in the stock market, including bonds, assets, and stock indexes. With more liquidity and less commission than other assets, ETFs trade more frequently over the course of the day, experiencing price fluctuations much like those experienced by stocks. In fact, other than the basic differences in their constitution, ETFs and stocks bear a striking resemblance in terms of the risks and trading opportunities. But over the long term, ETFs almost always trend in an upward direction. For this reason, they are favored by many long term investors.

But in the short term, ETFs are quite volatile, with periods of dropping prices almost always followed by massive growth. Identifying the right ETF is critical. The right one should be in high demand to ensure maximum liquidity to make it easy to buy and sell it. ETFs comprising of stocks from the tech sector are especially suitable because demand for tech stocks is high. However, you should keep in mind that an ETF will never be quite as volatile as a stock. The highs don't go very high and the lows are not as low. This is both good and bad. Good because your capital will not be eroded too much during a downswing and bad because the money you make from the price hikes won't be that high.

Cryptocurrency

Electronically mined and exchanged cryptocurrency has gained widespread prominence in the financial market as a possible replacement for the fiat currency currently in use. The adoption rate for these kinds of currency has been growing gradually, driven by, among other things, an unregulated environment. Bitcoin is one of the most popular cryptocurrencies, and one whose adoption rate has been quite high.

The unpredictable nature of cryptocurrency makes it very volatile. On the one hand, crypto could be the future of the economy, enabling people to move value virtually anywhere in the world. On the other, government policies and regulations could just as easily kill them off or make it too difficult to exchange commodities and services using them. Even though the volatility of Bitcoin does not yet have an index, it has been known to change up to ten times compared to the US dollar in a short time.

Any time there is good news about the adoption rate, like a popular retailer accepting cryptocurrency, prices skyrocket. Bad news articles have the opposite effect on the value. Other things to look out for include the future of crypto, security breaches and strengthened security parameters, high profile losses or gains, and government regulations. In deciding whether or not an event is likely to send the price up or down, use your intuition to imagine how investors will react to the news.

With that being said, the high volatility of the crypto market is probably too much for beginner investors. It requires seasoned swing traders who have developed a feel for the overall swing trading environment to make the right prediction. Because while a loss with a stock or ETF will erode your investment, the massive volatility of cryptocurrency (up to 10 times) will probably wipe out your entire position if you get it wrong.

Forex

The Forex or foreign exchange market is basically the global market of currency exchange found in and representing every currency of every country in the world. More than $5 trillion worth of currencies are exchanged every day around the world, making Forex the biggest and most liquid financial asset ever. Like every other financial asset, Forex fluctuates with every trade based on the rules of supply and demand. Currency values traded against other currencies are ever fluctuating. On Monday at 10:05, you will buy a pound for 1.19 Euros. Three hours later, the price will be down to 1.16. The next day, it will probably have climbed to 1.20. International businesses that convert large volumes of money to take care of business needs across different currency zones have the greatest impact on the Forex market, but international travel also plays a part.

When swing trading Forex, we use fundamental and technical analysis to identify upswings. The best Forex markets are those that are very liquid, which means that the two currencies whose exchange rate you trade in must be strongly interlinked economically. This ensures that there is enough liquidity to facilitate your buy and sell orders. To make money as a swing trader, volatility is always your best friend. So look out for pairs whose exchange rate fluctuates regularly, within short periods of time, and with high enough values to make your transaction profitable.

Once everything is determined to be in place for a profitable trade, you simply buy a certain quantity of a currency like the Euro, using another one, like the US dollar and hold it until the price is right. You then simply sell at a higher price and make money on the margin!

Options

An option is a financial contract that gives the holder the right to buy an asset at a certain price and sell when another price is reached. The great thing about options is that they simply give you as the holder the right, but don't compel you to buy or sell if you don't want to. There are two types of options; call and put. A call option gives you as the holder the right (but, again, not the obligation) to buy a certain asset when it reaches a certain price in a specified time. For example, you can buy a call option allowing you to short sell Apple stock if it reaches 115% of its current price in the next two weeks from the day of buying the option. With a put option, you retain the right to sell an asset at any time in the future, either stated or price-determined. Options are perhaps the most flexible, versatile, and profitable financial assets available to the swing trader, especially because they have an expiration clause by which time you must have exercised your option. Options entail a see-saw kind of transaction, which is to say that for every bullish call option buyer there must be a bearish seller. Put options have bearish buyers and bullish sellers.

There is a very specific strategy to swing trading options. It starts with picking the right asset; one with a large percentage move backed by clearly visible fundamental causes. After identifying your stock, look out for the right market environment. When looking to buy a call option, a bullish trend is your assured bet to great profits and if you are targeting a put option, a bearish market works great. This cross-play in the suitability of option purchases makes them even more suitable as swing assets. There will always be an opportunity to swing trade, whether the market is in a bearish or bullish trend. The other strategy to employ when buying options is to buy on pullbacks. This means that you optimize your entry point and choose the best possible exits points. Lastly, don't take your eyes off the trade. The opportunity to exit may come at any time. The good thing is that with the resources discussed in the last chapter, you don't have to stay glued to your screen. Your scanners will send you an alert when your predetermined exit or entry point is reached.

Chapter 4: Fundamental Analysis

Fundamental analysis measures the real value of a stock using the financial statements to reveal whether a stock is overvalued or undervalued. By using fundamental analysis you gain an up-down and inside-out understanding of the stock by looking at the parent company, which is the real determinant of stock valuation. In fundamental analysis, we use ratios to get an idea of how sound a company is as an investment opportunity. On the other hand, technical analysis studies the stock market indications of a company, including the stock price, fluctuation patterns (and the reasons behind them), support and resistance points, and the stock market recognition of the stock's potential. Using these indications, you can predict, with a certain measure of confidence, the future price changes of a stock and position yourself accordingly to profit.

Technical analysis differs from fundamental breakdown on the prediction of future prices. While the former looks only at the stock market factors, the latter factors in the intrinsic value of the company. And while they both work, they are suited for different types of stock market operatives. With fundamental analysis and the evaluation of fair stock pricing, you ignore the market factor (the biggest determinant of stock prices) and make decisions based on reasoned analysis. And while stock prices ultimately settle back at or around the fair value, only the investor can afford to overlook the profit-making potential of a stock that swings upward based on market hype. Technical analysis focuses solely on these stock market factors and is thus suitable for the trader because their interest is solely on the current prices, not the ideal price, which could take months to manifest.

Fundamental indicators are very slow in responding to market factors. The smallest time frame for fundamental markers to change is the three-month period when companies release quarterly earnings. On the other hand, technical indicators like price, fluctuation patterns, and resistance points change by the minute. It is exceedingly hard to find a stock that remains with the same technical indicators for more than a day. In the course of one week, so much fluctuation will have been witnessed that a previously stellar trading opportunity could suddenly become very unfavorable.

With day trading, you can afford to completely ignore the fundamental indicators. The short time of holding a position means that they will hardly ever come into play for your transactions. In fact, day traders have created the principle of efficient market hypothesis, stating that whatever current price a stock exchanges for is the fair price. This allows traders to save precious time that would otherwise be used to determine the "ideal" price of a stock and instead carry out the technical analysis that predicts future prices. But with swing trading, it is absolutely necessary to run fundamental analysis on a stock before committing to the purchase.

Even though fundamental analysis is considered an investors' tool, swing traders can benefit from a thorough understanding of a company's fundamentals to predict upcoming surges and to avoid times when little or no activity takes place. And because in swing trading we only make money on upswings in prices and volatility (periods of massive trading activity when prices change by huge margins), fundamental analysis is all the more important.

Financial Ratios

The following five ratios are the most effective fundamental indicators of a stock's suitability as an investment opportunity; EPS, P/E, RoE, D/E, and cash flow.

Earnings Per Share

The earnings per share ratio indicates the profit allocation for every share of a company, using the total profits made in a business period and the outstanding shares issued. Stocks with huge EPS ratios are usually more lucrative, which means that their stock prices are often higher than their fair price.

As a swing trader, you can use the EPS ratio of a company and profit forecasts to determine a company whose stock price is likely to skyrocket after a favorable profits release in a few weeks' time. Usually, investors respond very enthusiastically to the stock of a company that just released great financial results immediately after the release, sending the stock into an upswing, which makes for a great profit-making opportunity for the prospecting swing trader.

Price to Earnings Ratio

The P/E ratio is used to determine the value the stock market places on a company's future earnings prospects. Stocks with higher P/E ratios represent overvalued companies and ones that enjoy massive investor confidence. Stocks with high P/E ratios are usually very volatile, changing prices within hours of any news item that paints the company positively or negatively. These are usually great swing trading opportunities.

Debt to Equity Ratio

Otherwise known as the risk ratio, the debt to equity ratio indicates the capital structure of a company. The liabilities of a company are weighted against the shareholder equity to indicate whether it is equity or debt based. Companies that can easily cover their liabilities with assets are considered to be good investment opportunities because they are still in control of their financial fortunes.

Return on Equity

The return on equity measures the potential of a company to reward stockholders with a good return per share. It is essentially an indication of how well the management of a company uses its assets to make money. Investors prefer companies with high RoE because there is greater confidence that their investment will pay off with a good return.

Cash Flow Ratio

The cash flow ratio calculates the ratio of current debts with the current assets (cash) accumulated over a short period of time. It measures the short term liquidity of a company. As such, companies that generate more cash with little debt are considered to be very ideal for investing and trading in.

All these ratios are crucial for swing traders to determine stocks that present a good trading opportunity, especially at and around the financial release season when companies announce their financial performance for the period ending at a certain time.

Chapter 5: Technical Analysis

Technical analysis is an area that overwhelms a lot of new traders. I mean, how do you deal with all those numbers? And it is all about charts and even more charts, which for some of us can become absolutely overwhelming. And anyway, why are there are so many of them? The idea is to create a clear mental image of the ideal points of the chart at which you can execute a profitable trade. This is the reason why you must recite charts over and over again, memorizing different patterns and storing them in the subconscious for recall when you need to execute a trade.

Psychology explains that even intuition, the tool that seasoned traders use to identify good entry points and the best exit points, is comprised of a store of experiences and our interpretation of them. The more trades you execute, the greater the store you are going to accumulate of profitable trades and the point of the stock price chart at which they were made.

Will it be hard? Yes, it probably will. Especially if you are not a numbers person, cramming all the charts and the values represented on them will be a very tasking undertaking. The good news is that most technical indicators are redundant. A whole lot of different charts are often used to explain the same thing in different ways. Evaluating them before making a trade decision will, therefore, be overkill that will generate little extra insight for you. Understanding what is important and what is fluff to keep traders feeling like they are conducting the due diligence tasks before committing to a trade, will probably save you a lot of time. Failure to recognize the points at which charts overlap will turn you into a chart memorizer rather than a trader. And with this risk will come another, more serious one; that you might miss a trading opportunity because you were too busy analyzing the same thing on the third chart. The first rule of swing trading profitably and making it stress-free is that you must cut down on the process of identifying and vetting stocks and focus on the execution of sales.

The single most repeated mistake by traders in the stock market is that of buying into resistance and selling into support. It is the mistake that hundreds of thousands of novice traders have made time and time again. And one after the other, these traders have lost large amounts of money, often without realizing their mistakes. On the other side of this story are the smart traders who make money from the mistakes of these hapless fellows.

In fact, every money-making strategy that you are going to learn in this book or any other about the financial market is an attempt to get you out of the losing group and into the section of those who get the money lost. For every profit-making trade, you will make, there will be another trader losing money. And at that moment when you actually lose some money (yes, it is bound to happen), someone will be laughing all the way to the bank while counting your hard-earned and hard-lost dollars. The reason why technical analysis is such a handy tool for traders can be explained by this single statement; traders profit from the mistakes of other traders. Every risk you talk yourself into making is a chance you take that your money will end up in someone else's pockets.

You see, the thing that has happened ever since the stock markets opened is that people flocked to them with the aim of making money. To make money, they had to protect themselves from risk. Charts seemed like they presented them with the best opportunity to shield themselves from losses while also making some profit. The fact that on the other side of the equation is another person trying to do the same thing is what makes the stock market, especially the trading part, so uncertain.

But if you can be bold and recognize that the charts are simply numbers driven by human emotions then you can realize that they are not all that unpredictable. I don't mean that you should stop analyzing charts. And this is not a license to go against the technical indicators that you can gather from a chart. But after all is said and done, recognize that charts are driven by humans and you will have the cheat codes you need to establish quite a successful swing trading operation. Yes, the secret to making it in the swing trading environment is to understand not just the driving forces behind financial asset performance, but also a thorough understanding of the people behind those upswings and plummets.

It might take you a couple of months to get the hang of it but in the end, you will have a huge advantage over other traders. This advantage will mean that where appropriate, the money lost by other traders will be lost to you. You must give yourself an advantage over other traders. If everyone has the skills of technical analysis down pat, give yourself an edge by combining them with people analyzing skills and use these skills to analyze the market. You don't have to work harder than everyone else. You just need to work smarter. But here is the thing; smarter starts off as exceptionally hard before becoming smart, simple, and easy.

One of the most effective ways to identify short-term trading opportunities is to look for a reversal using candlestick and oscillation charts. Oscillations can be shown using measures like the relative strength index; an indication of the strength of a stock identified from the closing stock prices of recent trading periods. They enable swing traders to identify how well a stock is doing on all technical indicators, which the stock price does not always cover.

Price reversals make for excellent starting points for a trade. A reversal is a point in the chart when the direction of a stock turns around and starts trending downward after a period of upward trending or upward movement reverses into downward trending.

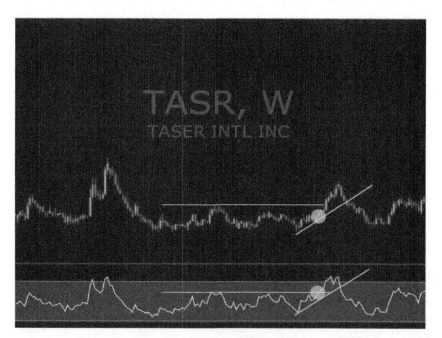

Chart 1: Stock price chart showing a point at which the trend of a stock chances into an upward direction (Speedtrader, 2019).

When trying to identify a moment of reversal, look out for the point at which a stock starts achieving lower lows and lower highs after trending upward or when its downward movement is reversed with higher lows and higher highs. It is important for you to learn to spot reversals because it allows you to identify an exit point that will allow you to make the most profit or the least loss. And when price reversals happen back to back, engulfment happens, causing price reversal to swallow up a previous one, either in an upward or downward direction.

Chart 2: Candlestick chart showing a bearish engulfment (Mitchell, 2018)

Another chart-reading skill is the identification of oscillator divergence, the point around which a decline or rise in stock price is foreshadowed by the aforementioned higher lows and higher highs (for a rise) and lower lows and lower highs (for a decline). By identifying these points, you can anticipate a rise in price or a decline. The chart below indicates the divergence point of Apple Inc. between the end of 2017 and early months of 2018. Notice the lower highs and lower lows between November and December 2017 which predicted the massive fall in price in February 2018.

Chart 3: Candlestick chart showing an incident of oscillator divergence (Mitchell, 2018)

For swing trading chart analysis, the candlestick and oscillator method comes in handy to help you identify impending reversals. Each method can be used alone, but combining them together is even more effective. By looking at the relative strength index against the price, you can identify a discrepancy and predict, with an average degree of accuracy, the most likely direction of the stock price. This is how swing traders identify stocks that can be good to buy when the rest of the stock market (looking only at the price) is shunning them. When the price reversal takes place, it brings with it a selling opportunity for the swing trader who then exits at a higher price and makes their money on the margin.

The fine science of technical analysis is too extensive for us to exhaust in this chapter. And because this is not a full technical analysis book, I recommend you check out "Trend Trading for Dummies" by Barry Burns. The book gives you the most in-depth analysis of technical analysis applicable to swing trading. This may seem counter-intuitive, but I recommend you DO NOT buy the "Technical Analysis for Dummies" book by Wiley books. The skills taught in that particular text will never take you beyond a layman's understanding of technical analysis, which is actually useless for a swing trader anyway. Barry Burns' book is dedicated specifically for swing traders.

Chapter 6: Trading Overnight Gaps

Now that we have established the ground rules, let's get on to the real stuff; the exact ways that a swing trader makes their money in the stock market. And while we are talking about the technical analysis of the stock market charts, exactly at what point are you supposed to buy and sell? Because the point which you enter and exit the market will determine whether you make it as a swing trader or if your losses will be the money that more intelligent traders than you will make their money from. This trader eat novice trader dynamic is indicated in the chart below.

Chart 4: The different entry and exit points for different types of traders (Swing-Trade-Stocks, 2019).

At point A, breakout traders buy into the stock as soon as the price starts rising. Here, there is no clear indication as to the direction the chart will be moving, so it is more of a gamble to buy at this point. The traders who pick this point are often the day traders who count on the "greater fool theory" to bring in novice traders, send the price climbing, and allow them to exit profitably.

With no clue what they are doing, the novice traders come in at point B, bringing in the money that the breakout traders will make their profits from. You would think that seeing the price as high as it is would dissuade the novice trader from entering the market at this point, but the novice's complete lack of awareness about the basic workings of the stock market becomes the saving grace of the breakout trader. And the stock market lives to see another price reversal.

At point C, momentum traders come in, buying from the last of the breakout traders (those who did not capture the novice traders at the higher price). With an intermediate understanding of the stock markets, momentum traders anticipate a likely price surge. And because momentum traders are also clueless about the price movements of the stock market, they put their stop-loss prices at the low of the hammer (point D). And now, as the price falls to a higher low, the market becomes ripe enough for more intelligent beings to enter.

At area E, the swing trader analyzes the charts and identifies the tell-tale signs of a stock about to hit its main high in the shortest time so far. Panicked novices and momentum traders sell en masse because the price fell below their stop-loss levels. With prices dropping and sell orders ballooning, the prices that were previously resistance points become supports. And now the swing trader does enter the market.

And because the stock has found a new support, the exiting momentum traders re-enter, increasing demand and send the price climbing to stratospheric new heights. At point F, the novice traders enter again. And once more, they choose the most unsuitable point to do so. The swing traders sell at the apex and leave them to their own means. If the price keeps rising for some reason (almost assuredly impossible), the novice will probably make money. The more likely scenario is that the novice traders simply come in to be the fodder from which the prospecting swing trader will make their huge profits.

Gaps

Sometimes, when the price of a financial asset is trending downward or upward, there are price ranges at which no trades are made. In the price chart, these price ranges appear as blank spaces known as gaps. Gaps may be intraday or overnight.

Intraday gaps happen when the stock trends in a downward or upward direction in the course of the trading hours but leave a gap at which point no transactions are executed. There are four types of intraday gaps; breakaway, continuation, exhaustion, and common.

With breakaway gaps, a stock will usually be trending in a certain course for a while, then it suddenly changes track and jumps into a different direction. Breakaways occur during price reversals, with the only distinction being that there is a price range when no transactions occur, but a different price a few points up or down sets the new price at which the stock will trade for the rest of the trading period. High volume trades triggered by an external event are usually responsible for this phenomenon.

Continuation gaps occur when a stock that is either rising or dropping in price skips a certain price range but continues in the same direction. When it occurs during an upward trend, a continuation gap represents a jump in investors' confidence levels. In the same way, a downward trend indicates dropping confidence levels.

And after an asset has trended in a certain direction for a while, there often occurs exhaustion gaps in which the price continues in the same course for a while before reversing and closing the gap. This distinction of a reversal that closes the gap is necessary for a reversed gap to be considered an exhaustion one.

The last type of gap is more of an anomaly than anything else. In the course of a trading day, a stock or other asset could jump in price shortly after making a sharp move. For example, an ETF that has been trending downward for the past four days then suddenly gaps upward creates a common gap. There is nothing to read from it since it is simply an anomaly.

On the other hand, overnight gaps occur when the price of an asset skips a certain range in trading between the previous day's close and the next day's opening price. There are two types of overnight gaps depending on the kind of market run the financial market is going through, namely up gaps or down gaps. Up gaps are formed when the highest price at which a stock closes one day is lower than the next day's opening price. The price then retains the upward trend, being a part of a bullish market.

The inverse gap formation is called a down gap. It takes place in a bearish market and usually happens when the market closes at a low price, but it opens at an even lower price whilst skipping a few price points. The asset then trades below the previous day's low point for the entire day and closes below it.

How to Trade Gaps

Gaps present a profit-making opportunity for enterprising traders because they indicate certain technical or fundamental conditions. In the stock market, the overnight upward gap is caused very often by company earnings results being higher than expected. A lot of businesses have taken to announcing earnings results after the close of trading in the stock market to avoid too much market shock. With good results, investor confidence rises sharply, causes a spike in the bid and ask spread, and makes the next day's opening price to be significantly higher than the previous day's closing. Technical factors also cause overnight gapping, like when a stock breaks new highs during the day. Day traders, keen on cashing in on the high prices, scramble to buy the stock the next day at a price higher than the previous day's close. This creates a technical gap.

But exactly how do you make money on the gaps? The rule of trading gaps is very simple. You should buy after a wave of selling and sell after a wave of buying. This simple strategy ensures that when you buy, the prices are really low because the supply exceeds the demand. By the time you come around to selling after the buying wave, the price will be high enough to give you a nice profit. Amateur traders do the exact opposite. They see a stock advancing in price and are afraid that they will miss out on the move, so they pile in - just when the pros are getting ready to sell. In a way, this dynamic allows the financial markets to maintain an equilibrium.

When thinking about trading gaps, you should keep in mind that most of them always get filled. Other than continuation and breakaway gaps that are used to confirm a certain price trend, the price will usually change and rebalance after a while to fill the gap. Understanding this fact will help you determine the best position to take after a gap has occurred. So, swing traders usually buy at the lowest prices and wait for the market to correct the gap, making money on the whole range of the gap or choosing to go halfway just to be safe. Even though the massive price jump means that there is usually no support or resistance for the new price, you can still set a stop-loss price. So if you plan to sell at 50% of the gap, you can set the stop loss 50 percentage points away from your entry point. In those rare cases when the price doesn't reverse even briefly to cover the gap, or when the gap gets filled but not all the way through, a different kind of gap called the follow-through gap will usually form in the near future.

Another strategy that some seasoned swing traders use, especially in bull markets, is to wait for the gap to be filled before committing to trade the asset. Here, traders make their judgment based on the expectation that the price will follow the trend and continue rising. This strategy is perhaps safer because there is a reliable support/resistance price level, so you can set up your stop loss with some level of confidence.

When the price of an asset reverses and fills a gap that occurred on the same day, it is said to have faded the gap. This often happens in the earnings season when many companies announce their financial results. The market exuberance at this time is usually high, which gives way to lots of irrational trading activity.

Examples of Gap Trades

Let's look at a few examples of gap trades to give you a better idea of how it all works. The most commonly used gap trading strategy is one where a trader buys stocks in after-hours trading because a company just announced favorable financial results. The next morning, as the rest of the stock market opens, the price gaps a few points, allowing the trader to pull out of the trade before the market starts to fill the gap. As an example, consider a scenario when Walmart closed the day at $90.22 on the day that the company was expected to release its financial results. The retail sector had not been doing all that well, so there was widespread speculation, with public opinion leaning towards an expectation of unfavorable or mediocre earnings reports. But it was still anyone's guess what kind of profits America's biggest brick and mortar retailer would post and until the results were actually released, the direction of the stock was unpredictable.

If, in this case, a prospecting swing trader with all the right scanning tools recognized a possible price upsurge and received an alert from Scoop Markets with an analysis showing that Wal-Mart's earnings reports were likely to be even better than anticipated, logic dictates that they position themselves to benefit. As for our case, swing traders bought during a downward surge just before the market closed. A few hours later, the results were out. Profits were higher than expected and all other fundamentals were quite acceptable. As the markets opened the following day, excitement among investors was at fever pitch, with buy orders flooding during the pre-market session and early trading session. Just as expected, a massive gap formed. The next day's first stocks started at $98.64, which, at 9.3%, represented a sizeable gap profit for the swing trader to make a good profit off of, even if they didn't wait for the price to climb higher.

The above example represents an up gap. It happens when prices are rising from previous prices and skipping a price upward. So how do you make money if the stock is dropping and skipping a price range but in a downward direction? Well, you have the concept of short selling to thank for that. In short selling, you take a stock position when you are sure that the price is going to come down by borrowing a number of stocks at a future low price (set at the time, price, or left open to the short seller's discretion) from a broker. The current price becomes the selling point, which means that you will make more money the lower the stock price falls. Short selling a gap trade just makes your profit larger because your stock skips a price range on its downward trend. When looking for down gap stocks to swing trade, the best place to look is in a company that is going through some serious crisis.

From a careful fundamental analysis of Tesla Inc., you will discover that the stock is grossly overvalued. The company's price to book value ratio stands at the 8 point range, which is more than three times the value considered to be safe for value investors. And because the company has been facing serious financial and leadership issues, investor confidence has been eroding massively as the company missed production targets and continued to call back Model 3 cars due to defective fuel cells among other issues, the stock has been going down in value for quite some time now. In January 18, 2019, Tesla experienced a gap down of a spectacular 8.4% from the previous day's closing price after CEO Elon Musk announced that the company planned to lay off about 7% of its workforce. With the tweet posted at about 6:45 AM, pre-market traders had about two and a half hours to short-sell the stock before the normal trading hours started and the down gap happened. Swing traders who use the Twitter-based Scoop Markets received notifications of the news hours before the rest of the market, allowing them to short-sell massive volumes of Tesla stock and, a few hours later, make a killing when the prices dropped by more than $20.

An innumerable number of short sells have also been made on the Forex markets basically any time there is negative news about a country. The weekend no-trading season is especially notorious as a watershed for Monday morning down gaps. From Brexit to the Greece elections, suddenly depreciating currencies have created numerous profitable swing trades in the Forex markets since time immemorial. The explanation for the heavy gapping that occurs in the Forex markets is simply that currencies are very dependent on geopolitical factors for stability. And because political matters are ever-shifting, currencies are always losing value against others. If you decide to swing trade Forex market gaps, just remember to keep this fact in mind; short sell the affected currency on bad news and long sell when the news is positive. Trading the exchange rate against the US dollar works best because it is the universal standard and thus very liquid.

Chapter 7: Hot Sector Mania

While the mainstream financial assets market is usually the preserve of the investment savvy individual and just a few novice traders, any time there is some excitement about a particular asset it becomes an opportunity for hangers-on to join the gravy train in the promise of a quick buck. As we saw above, these people come in when the prices are very high because the trending item is, well, trending. Without concern for supports, resistance, or fundamental and technical analysis, novices break open their savings accounts, sell off assets, even take loans, to avoid being left behind. It is actually from hot sectors that bubbles form. And bubbles are also quite opportune themselves!

You see, hot sectors and bubbles attract euphoric interest in the financial markets for the non-trading public. The fear of missing out motivates their buying decisions and overpowers their common sense, making them commit massive amounts of money en masse. This is the worst thing you can do as a swing trader. You see, unlike these one-off or sporadic traders, you cannot afford to lose money this carelessly. It wouldn't be a very profitable operation you would be running if you did not do your due diligence before committing your money or if you joined every hot market at any point. And unlike other investment self-help books that advise against hot markets, I am not about to say that you should keep off. Oh no! My advice is actually on the contrary, actually; you should seek out hot sectors. Just be careful to choose your entry and exit points properly, because hot sectors can be very profitable or very risky.

Hot sectors are very great trading opportunities for four very simple reasons. First, they bring massive demand. As the first investors come in and make a killing from a hitherto vanilla sector, the rest of the market responds favorably. Along with the financial markets, media, blogs, social media, and word of mouth takes the new opportunities wide. Stories of "people like you" making hundreds of thousands within a few weeks or months propel demand sky high. The massive demand has the double-edged effect of making prices rise and increasing the demand for the asset. It thus becomes very easy to buy and sell an asset.

Secondly, even though the public gets very interested and buys en masse into a financial product, the least bit of concern expressed by any analyst or unsuccessful participant creates widespread panic selling. For the seasoned trader who can determine if the hot sector is still in the awareness or stealth phase, this kind of selling presents a wonderful swing trading opportunity. By the principle of gap trading espoused in the last chapter, you should buy after a wave of selling and sell after a wave of buying. As the media interest in a hot sector drives demand up and down every so often, every downswing presents a buying moment and every upswing a selling (read profit making) opportunity.

The third reason why hot sectors are great swing trading opportunities is because of the volume of trades that take place every day. Volume trades ensure that your sell order never goes unfilled by more than just a few minutes, making it easier to make numerous trades in a short time whenever the chance becomes available.

Finally, and this is the biggie, hot sectors are excellent trading opportunities because there are so many more novice traders attempting to join them. Ensnared by the promise of quick money, the public floods into hot sectors, bringing with it massive amounts of capital, a fair share of which seasoned traders ensnare. This is not to say that novice traders don't make any money from hot sectors. Some of them are able to crack the concept of going against the market and actually make money, but the majority are scared when prices drop and excited when they rise. Selling in the former and buying in the latter, they practically give out their dollars and buy them back at lower prices from professional traders.

And there you go. Four simple reasons why you should totally swing trade hot sectors and crush it. But be careful. Greed could get to you and take you into the bull trap that marks the boundary between the mania phase (money making) and the blow-off phase when process free fall and turns all four reasons to trade the hot sectors into nightmares of trading in a cooling hot sector or bursting bubble. The massive demand turns into heavy supply which conspires with the volume SELL orders of panicked amateur traders and sends prices plummeting so fast you won't have anywhere to hold on to. That is unless you short sold the hot asset close to the free-fall price level. But sometimes even the short sell order may not materialize because no one is interested in buying an asset that has just had its bubble burst.

Historical Hot Sectors

The financial market has seen numerous hot sectors rise and fall. Sometimes it is simply a single stock, sometimes it is an asset class. In this sector, we are going to look at hot sectors of the economy that have captured the attention of the public. They include the dotcom boom (internet companies), the cryptocurrency bubble, biotech companies, and marijuana (a commodity whose value is pegged on companies that supply it). Buckle up people, its story time.

The Dotcom Boom

The first internet browser, Mosaic web browser, was released to the public in 1993. It brought with it a fantastic new invention- the internet. The American home had just previously been revolutionized with a great new invention- the personal computer- and the ability to access an ever-increasing database of information and send some at the touch of a button created massive demand.

Mosaic web browser was the brainchild of Netscape Communications Corporation, the latter of whom made their IPO in 1995. The IPO was wildly successful, as was Yahoo!'s a few months later. As other internet companies set up to offer consumers with internet peripherals and applications, the internet sector soon became the most profitable segment of the stock market. As major beneficiaries of initial public offerings, investment banks fueled speculation in the technology sector. The result was that a company simply had to have .com in its name to become an overnight hit in the stock market.

By 1999, some technology shares were up over 1,000%. Yes, those were three zeroes. And like in every hot sector, the public played a key role in the development of the dotcom bubble. Some people actually quit their jobs to day trade full time. By this point, the venture capitalists who had poured money into openly unsustainable internet start-ups were selling out en masse. See, it is always the hapless public that gets screwed over in the end.

The technology sector cooled down rapidly starting in early 2000 when the Fed raised interest rates and by the end of 2002, the bubble had burst. In the end, $5 trillion from 401K plans and savings accounts had been wiped from the buying public. And because every single dollar exchanged hands and went to another person, this also means that professional traders and investors who were clever enough to exit the market before the bubble burst collectively made $5 trillion.

Even today, baby boomers (the generation that was most involved in the dotcom boom) complain that the economy of America is skewed in favor of the elite. There is no such thing. There are only the people who learn to play the markets and those who follow the hottest trends and end up lining the pockets of the former with their hard-earned cash. It is entirely up to you what side of that equation you end up on.

The Cryptocurrency Boom

The development of virtual currencies started years ago, but it was not until Bitcoin broke the $1000 barrier for the first time in 2013 that cryptocurrency really grabbed the attention of the world. As a decentralized means of digital exchange of value created using blockchain technology, Bitcoin presented investors everywhere with the means to transact on the internet without leaving a paper or electronic trail. Cryptocurrencies are created through programming code using cryptography technology. To the public, cryptocurrencies are issued through an Initial Coin Offer (ICO), which also sets their exchange price measured against fiat currencies.

Even though numerous other cryptocurrencies were issued to the public starting from 2009, Bitcoin would gain prominence as the most mainstream. So much so that other crypto coins were referred to, in some quarters, as alternative digital currencies or altcoins. Without going into the specifics of cryptocurrency operations, suffice it to say that despite concerns over the unregulated nature of cryptocurrency, Bitcoin and other currencies grew very popular in the 2010s. A bullish investor mindset had driven prices up all through the decade, with price hikes persevering through numerous hacking cases in which bitcoin exchanges were targeted and prices plunged. The result; the price of one Bitcoin had reached close to $20,000 by the end of 2017 after starting off at less than $0.003 eight years previously. And then the crash happened, plunging the price down 80% to about $4,000. So what exactly happened?

The reckoning of the cryptocurrency market started way back in December 2017 when one of Bitcoin's founders announced that he would be selling his stake in Bitcoin. This resulted in a 45% drop in the price of Bitcoin as well as other currencies. It is worth noting at this point, that Bitcoin almost single-handedly carries the identity of cryptocurrency. The trends set by Bitcoin spread across the whole cryptocurrency market. Less than a month later, the government of South Korea announced that it was considering halting the buying and selling of cryptocurrency in the country. Coming in the wake of the previous plunge, this announcement sent the price of Bitcoin down another 12%. As world governments started taking notice of this bold new currency that threatened existing fiat money, state legislation in Texas and North Carolina in America sent prices plummeting 92% in just a few days. A few price adjustments would happen in the course of the year 2018 before Bitcoin settled at its $4,000 rock bottom price.

Today, a single Bitcoin trades for $9,000 and is still considered a hot sector. The massive volatility indicates great demand and just like the dotcom bubble burst, the cryptocurrency crash of 2009 wiped massive value off cryptocurrency but still left something to grow back. In fact, the 2009 crash can be seen as the maturity of cryptocurrency. After the initial euphoric interest, Bitcoin and other currencies have been growing steadily ever since, with an ever-increasing adoption rate among mainstream commercial institutions.

And just because it is a largely untested financial asset does not mean that Bitcoin has no trading value. As a pioneering financial tool, cryptocurrency is highly volatile, with any positive news driving prices up and negative media coverage shaving prices quite massively. All-round, Bitcoin and other types of cryptocurrencies are worth keeping an eye on for any enterprising swing trader.

Biotech

Humans have been modifying living organisms for their own good since they started domesticating animals. Modern biotechnology entails the artificial selection and hybridization of living cells to create superior plant and animal offspring, a practice that has birthed a whole new sector known collectively as the biotech industry. A company in the biotech industry uses living organisms like enzymes and bacteria to make drug and supplementary health products. Biotech competes directly with the pharmaceutical industry, which uses artificially produced chemicals. The biotech industry is another sector that is currently going through a massive boom.

The biotech bubble, boom, or opportunity has bamboozled investors since around 2015 when *Time Magazine* ran a story predicting that the biotech 'bubble' may finally have popped. The speculation was caused by a valid observation that the stocks of biotechnology companies had been behaving in much the same way that internet startups were acting in the 1990s. IPOs of even the youngest venture capital-backed biotech firms have been many, oversubscribed, and quite unreasonable. In some cases, companies with no definitive plans to release a drug have received massive interest from investors. Between 2012 and 2015, the NASDAQ Biotechnology Index had risen 177% against an overall stock market growth of 52% as measured by the Standard & Poor 500 Index.

But fast forward to 2019 and the biotech sector is still as hot as it was five years ago, perhaps even hotter now that it has proven itself capable of withstanding serious tempests and price declines. Perhaps it is because the healthcare industry is considered a defensive sector, but something keeps the biotech industry propped even after going through bubble-bursting triggers. In 2015, several biotech companies were accused of blatantly rising drug prices. There was even the threat of political fallout when the then prospective Democratic Presidential candidate Hillary Clinton in a tweet labeled the pricing strategies of biotech companies outrageous. Democratic lawmakers picked up the call and threatened to open a congressional inquiry into the profiteering ways of some companies. In highly leveraged booming sectors, a single tweet like that would be enough to bring a downward spiral that would burst a bubble. But the NASDAQ Biotechnology Index lost a measly 6% before picking up after a while.

As the stock market remains unsure about the fate of the biotech industry and fears that a bubble is forming abound, the sector remains quite volatile. This makes it a prime candidate for swing trading, especially with bullish investor confidence keeping the demand for stocks sky high.

Marijuana Boom

Once, a long time ago, marijuana was considered to be a harmful drug. It was controlled by strict federal and state laws, with any use labeled a prosecutable criminal offense. But fast forward to 2019 and more than 33 states have decriminalized the use of marijuana for medical purposes. Of these, 10 have legalized recreational use of cannabis. This includes Washington, DC, the seat of the federal government, even though the federal government remains astutely opposed to marijuana use.

As more states have enacted legislation decriminalizing the use of marijuana for medicinal purposes, companies that deal in the growing, harvesting, processing, and distribution of marijuana-based drugs have gained widespread recognition. In states where it is legal, marijuana clinics contend for retail space with Laundromats and bodegas. And even though pot companies have just recently started trading in the major stock markets in America (February 2018 for NASDAQ and May of the same year for the NYSE), their stocks have been well subscribed, especially among the minority buyers. But as biotech companies start expressing interest in cannabinoid (from cannabis) agents in their drugs, marijuana stocks are bound to move from the over the counter (OTC) penny stock section where most of them are found and into the mainstream.

The marijuana boom is as much a commodity boom as it is a stock market one. The product itself is becoming more widely demanded, with companies like Canopy Growth Corp., Cronos Group Inc., Aurora Cannabis Inc., and Terra Tech Corp engaging in massive marketing and advocacy efforts all over the country. A number of other businesses in the biotech sector have also come up, including AbbVie, Cara Therapeutics, GW Pharmaceuticals, Axim Biotechnologies among others. All of these companies are in various stages of the clinical drug development process. Ancillary businesses have also emerged to service the marijuana enterprises, with some of the most prominent being Kushco Holdings, The Scotts Miracle-Gro Company, and GrowGeneration Corp. Other than these mainstream marijuana businesses, traditional vice companies like tobacco and beer have been disrupted and rejuvenated by the marijuana boom.

Obviously, this is just an early industry. We are yet to see how far it can go but the amount of interest generated, not just in the IPOs of marijuana companies but in the sector itself, indicates massive interest.

The Long-Island Iced Tea Company

The story of the Long-Island Iced Tea Corp. begs a single question; "What is in a name?" Facing waning financial fortunes and threats of delisting from the NASDAQ because of a low capitalization, the company's management came up with an ingenious idea to bolster their market cap without spending years on a corporate turnaround strategy- to change their name. Usually, a name change does not serve as a stimulus for low capitalization. But in this case, the new name the company adopted played right into a very hot sector-cryptocurrency. And so in December 2017, Long Island Iced Tea Company became Long Blockchain Corp. Immediately the price shot upward, rising an incredible 289% within a few weeks.

All this based on name only and a few vague promises to acquire cryptocurrency rigs and start mining Bitcoin. So how could a whole corporate entity become a victim of hype? Well, it fell for the same old euphoria that millions of Americans have fallen for in the numerous bubbles that have formed since the stock markets started. And like every investor that ever became fodder for more experienced traders, poor timing had a lot to do with their phenomenal mess. You see, shortly after the company announced their name change and witnessed the spectacular stock price surge, the whole cryptocurrency market collapsed and fell 80% by the end of the year. The Long Island Iced Tea Company was now judged as a confused beverage maker rather than a bold business diversifying to shield against market risks.

Sad as the story is, it indicates how fallible prices in the financial market can be. Even though a simple name change sent the price skyrocketing, the poor reasoning behind the whole idea could not sustain them. Hot sectors follow more or less the same principles; market hype may boost demand and drive up prices, but ultimately the fundamentals win out. Everything balances out.

Which brings us to this chapter's **Golden Rule.** If it looks too good to be true, then it probably is. Hot sector mania does not last. The profits that entice novice traders to join the market at the worst possible time become someone else's profits. So keep your eyes open and your wits around you. You are going to need both to become a versatile swing trader.

Chapter 8: How to Use Social Media to Spot Short-Term Opportunities

In 2019, social media penetration stands at about 3.5 billion, which is about 45% of the whole world population. And with this massive penetration, social media has caused disruption everywhere; personal relations, business, information transmission, and the mass media. An ever increasing number of people rely on social media for their news, counting on their connections around the world for live photos, commentary, and updates. In the past decade, breaking news no longer come from over-excited news reporters on TV over a large red BREAKING NEWS banner. Well, they do, but people don't rely on that to stay updated. Because by the time the station gathers its technical team, writing team, and make-up team to piece a new piece of information together and go to live broadcast, someone will probably have taken pictures and shared them all over social media.

And this new invention is bringing about massive changes in the way we get informed (and sometimes misinformed) about events. In the 2012 London Olympic Games, the NBC network decided to air delayed footage highlighting the most momentous events of the day rather than airing it live because attendees were posting so many pictures and commentary on social media that live coverage was considered redundant. In another case, social media users were first to know about the death of pop star Whitney Houston. And the raid that killed Osama Bin Laden was live-tweeted by a hapless Twitter user Sohaib Athar nine hours before the world was informed.

The most prominent social networking sites where news can often be found include Facebook, Twitter, Instagram, Snapchat, and others. But Twitter, with its character restriction and more structured interface, has gained prominence as somewhat of a news aggregation site. A simple scroll down the trending topics will promptly inform you what everyone around the world is currently excited about. And following the right influencers will bring a huge difference to your timeline. As an aspiring swing trader, that could be the difference between establishing a successful trading career and floundering.

You see, the world started noticing the impact of social media on consumer behavior, business interests, and commercial interests back in 2011 when conScore determined that social media, led by Facebook, was becoming the most influential online resource. The global investment markets were also disrupted by the rising prominence of social media. Where news would take hours to move from the source to the news stations before arriving to the viewing public and taking its toll on the stock markets, social media cut the process by half, allowing influencers to communicate directly to the public. A company could thus send a media release to news stations and post an update on social media, cutting down the impact time by a large margin.

As you start your swing trading journey, you should definitely keep social media as a part of your intelligence-gathering framework. Breaking news on social media that is momentous enough to make it to the mainstream will always bring about a shift in the financial asset involved, one way or another. But because not every trader takes full advantage of social media to collect information, it will give you a definite edge.

Traders to Follow on Twitter

But even more important is the role that social media plays in the education of new traders on trading techniques. There are quite a number of accounts of credible traders on Twitter and StockTwits that could turn out to be very informative. In this section, we look at the 10 best traders on Twitter. However, as you look for role models on social media, be wary of scammers and SPAM accounts that only seem to be interested in getting you to sign up for subscriptions and other commitments. Some of the advantages of following experienced traders on Twitter are that they will always give links to other resources, like websites where you can find more educational material, even while you follow their posts and trading activities.

However, let me take this opportunity to say that I can only verify the usefulness of the traders discussed below as of the writing of this book (June 2019). These are individuals and sometimes trading firms behind each account and unfortunately, people change and go rogue. I do not endorse these accounts; I merely listed the 10 most useful Twitter accounts I recommend you follow. Analyze each one as thoroughly as possible and follow only those which you think meet YOUR standards and will help you reach your trading GOALS.

@IncredibleTrade

This Twitter account doubles as the Twitter handle of the trading support website by the same name. The account states straight out that it does not encourage traders to buy or sell based on the tweets that are posted, and it has an uncluttered feel that inspires confidence. You will receive news from the timeline, but you can always link into the website (link provided, but no prompt) to see what they are all about. And Incredible Trades is all about the transmission of trading opportunities. The blog itself is clean and straight to the point. You can opt to sign up for a membership, which is rather on the expensive side, and receive notifications on your private Twitter news feed, email, or SMS. Unfortunately, other than the Twitter news feed, the blog offers little content for free members. But you can count on the tweets themselves being quite good, to the point, and well researched.

@PeterLBrandt

The @PeterLBrandt Twitter account is a personal brand of Peter Brandt, who calls himself a classical chart trader since 1980. With a #1 Amazon bestselling book under his belt, we can say that Brandt is a seasoned trader. His seeming obsession with charts and the art of chart analysis for the serious stock trader makes his Twitter handle a great place to start if you are hoping to learn all about charts and how to read them. The similarly named website gives you access to a ton of materials Brandt has created for his students, including a large cache of videos, a few books, and the chance to join webinars and master classes offered from time to time. The website also hosts Factor trading services, the research arm of Peter Brandt that generates market insights for users. Signing up to the Factor Service membership will cost you a few hundred bucks a year, but it will give you greater access to all these materials and other services like private Twitter feeds, alerts, and intelligence on the financial markets.

@SJosephBurns

Steve Burns is another veteran of the financial markets, having started his trading career in 1993. After transitioning to self-employment in 1995, he went on to found New Trader U, a trading website you can visit right from his profile, in 2011. He states on his bio that he tweets about trading, the financial markets, and the process of attaining financial freedom. He also tweets motivational quotes and pictures. Of all traders reviewed so far, Burns' website has the best free educational materials. It is also refreshed daily with new content on current market trends, chart analysis, and informative speculation. The website also unobtrusively offers numerous links to other resources on affiliated blogs as well as a listing of online courses and great books on the financial markets.

@AswathDamodaran

When you think Aswath Damodaran, the first thing that should come to mind should be corporate valuation. This New York University Stern School of Business professor of corporate finance and valuation tweets almost exclusively about valuation. His website is clunky and quite dull, with a busy outlay and hard-to-follow archival system. Which is a huge pity, because Professor Aswath Damodaran knows his valuation, loves to teach it, and has written loads of articles, books, and spreadsheets about it. He has also taught it at the Master's level. Or so he says, it is hard to tell from the landing page if the website is not simply a half-hearted attempt at digitization by a peripheral company in a peripheral sector of the economy. But if you can look beyond the terrible user interface, the website delivers what it promises to deliver and then some. For any trader looking to teach themselves more about valuation, Professor Aswath Damodaran's Twitter feed and website are definitely worth checking out.

@50Pips

50 Pips posts tweets about price action, market psychology, and asymmetric opportunities. They also operate a website by the same name (link on bio) where they offer educational webinars and video updates. Even though the people behind the website are unidentified and the website is in all caps (you don't realize how aesthetic small caps is until you are staring at a page written exclusively in caps), they do have a good blog, with a chart of the day that can be quite helpful if you are looking to absorb a ton of information quickly after a long day at work.

@alphatrends

@alphatrends is the Twitter handle of alphatrends.net, the brainchild of author and technical analysis guru Brian Shannon. With a mix of technical charts, breaking news alerts, and a motivational quote here and there, a visit to @alphatrends will always be worth it. And while you are there, duck into the website and check out their market analysis videos, classes, webinars, and books. Because this is one of the few outstanding traders who recognizes the power of swing trading really well. As a veteran, he will have a few ideas to share with you and teach you how to develop your own trading technique. With a membership in the website's Swing Traders' Forum, you will also receive a trade list of all stocks that have potential for swing trading.

@ukarlewitz

This Twitter account sets itself apart with almost exclusive coverage of the Standard & Poor 500 Index. If you can't make head or tail of the SPX, then @ukarlewitz is the Twitter feed to haunt. But apart from that, this rather eccentric trader who prides himself in being blocked by Zero Hedge since 2010 will post news about matters like the federal rates in the context of the financial markets. His BlogSpot site is also brim filled with S&P 500 analysis.

@option_snipper

The option sniper teaches followers the rules of picking out the most profitable options, among other things. The posts are more speculative than any other Twitter handle in this list, with quite an informative take on pretty much every geopolitical issue that affects the options markets. Follow @option_snipper for a variety of fringe and mainstream news on national and global events and how these events are likely to affect the financial markets.

@LMT978

First off, @LMT978 is a private account, so you will have to follow it just to view the complete profile. And when you have sent the request to follow him, maybe he decides you are not good enough to follow him and does not approve of your request. But he has been trading for 22 years and seems like a nice guy.

@OptionsHawk

@OptionsHawk presents visitors with the best options analytics of any trader listed here. The Twitter feed will keep you updated on not just the most recent developments in the financial markets; it will bring to your timeline financial news articles that are likely to affect stock, options, and Forex markets. In the website, you will have the option to pay a couple hundred dollars to receive products like spotlight trades, a spreadsheet of options to look out for, and a database of notable options that you might be interested to trade.

Social media is definitely an asset when you are trying to establish yourself as a trader. News breaks out on Twitter long before the public gets wind of it from the mainstream media. Scanners like Scoop Markets will send you alerts when something spectacular happens but if you are going to get on Twitter anyway, why not make every social media moment a moment of learning and empowering yourself as a swing trader? Following the people who matter in asset trading is the way to upgrade your timeline and saturate your life with trading expertise. And you can get this information from other social networking sites like Facebook too; it is all about the people you follow. Follow the right people and the information will come swarming into your life.

However, keep in mind that social media should be used as a resource and not your entire trading strategy. In fact, the only way that social media can be really reliable as an asset in your trading enterprise is when you combine it with other social media resources like Scoop Markets. This way, you don't have to spend all day scanning your timeline for actionable updates.

Chapter 9: Entry & Exit Strategies

Whatever else you learn about swing trading, remember that it all boils down to this, entry and exit points. In swing trading, the entry point is the price point at which you buy a stock, otherwise known as taking a position. You hold the position for a while and then sell when the conditions are right, which marks your exit point. Making a profitable swing trade is simply a matter of ensuring that your entry point is higher than your exit point when selling long. When short selling, just ensure that you exit at a lower price than you entered the trade. Easy, right? Well, the actual process is somewhat more complicated. You see the selection of the right entry and exit point in professional swing trading relies on a very precise set of technical analysis tools that help traders identify price patterns and predict future markets.

Basic Price Patterns

We have already touched on some of these tools, but it bears revisiting these points for clarity. But first, we need to define a few terms that you need to understand before you start analyzing price charts to identify entry and exit point. The first is **support**, which is basically the price which an asset rarely goes below. The support price goes up and down in tandem with the upward or downward movement in the price of an asset. The other term that you need to be able to identify is the **resistance**. This denotes the highest price an asset reaches before falling back down. These two price points are reversed by an increasing number of buyers and sellers respectively. The **pivot** is calculated as the average value of the previous day's closing, highest, and lowest prices. When the price trends above the pivot, it indicates a bullish market. Prices below a pivot indicate a bearish market.

Finally, the **trend line** is the visual representation of price movement. It is drawn from the pivot, resistance, and support prices and help traders analyze movement over time. By identifying the direction of a stock, you can detect an asset that has the potential for a good profit. Simply by observing whether the price is trending upward or downward over a given time; minutes, hours, days, or weeks, you can decide whether to buy or short sell a stock at that point.

But we all know that forecasting the direction of a financial asset is more complicated than that, simply because prices fluctuate over time. So looking at the trend alone does not quite give us all the information we need. This is why we also look at reversal and continuation patterns as well.

Reversal

Reversal is the adjustment in the direction of an asset's trend line. However, a lot more than a simple change in the direction of an asset price takes place at a reversal point. Aspects like the moving average, which determines the average price of an asset over time, come into bearing. Downward reversals happen when the moving average falls below the current price levels while upward reversals indicate that the moving average is growing higher.

Swing points predict reversals and help traders determine whether they should buy long or short sell a particular stock. An asset that is about to reverse downward swings high at first, then climbs even higher before falling to a lower high. They are perfect for short selling. An asset at the brink of reversing upward swings low then falls lower before rising to a higher low. It indicates an opportunity to buy long.

Continuation

Continuation happens as a result of a brief pause followed by persistence of the price of an asset. There are several types of continuation patterns, including triangles, pennants, flags, and rectangles.

- Triangles form when the resistance and support trend in opposite directions over a period of about three weeks. They can be symmetrical or have a descending or ascending slope.

- Pennants are smaller triangles formed when the resistance and support points travel in opposite directions for a period of 20 days or less.

- Flags are formed when short term support and resistance lines drawn between two or more price points create a parallel line. Flags indicate a high chance of volatility in that particular direction.

- Finally, rectangles form at the point where a pause is preceded or succeeded by a sideways trend in the direction of the price. When they appear in any sort of trend line (ascending, descending, or sideways), then it means that the trend will continue over the long term.

Heads and Shoulders

Heads and shoulders price patterns occur when a series of price movement is accomplished. An initial rise in price creates a shoulder, which then falls before rising higher than the first peak. A reversal happens at the peak, with the price falling lower than the first peak before shooting to the same price of the first peak to complete the shoulder-head-shoulder look of the head and shoulders price pattern. The head and shoulders pattern indicates a reversal of the market from bearish to bullish or the other way around.

Double Top/Bottom

Another price pattern is the double top/bottom. The double top occurs when the market tries unsuccessfully to pierce through a resistance point. It looks like the letter M and ends in a reversal, with the price moving downward. The double bottom occurs when the market makes two attempts to break through the support level but is unsuccessful. The reversal, in this case, leads to an upward movement. A rarer version of the double top/bottom is the triple top/bottom. It is a very powerful indication of an impending reversal.

The final price pattern you can look out for before determining the best entry point in a swing trade is the gap. But since we have discussed gaps extensively in an earlier topic, let me just reiterate that the gap is the only price pattern that is caused by external factors. The rest of the price patterns are only identifiable by technical analysis, but gaps are caused by fundamental analysis. The only way to predict a gap is to keep your ear to the ground.

The graph below indicates all the price patterns discussed above. It is meant to guide you in identifying them in a price chart and is purely demonstrational.

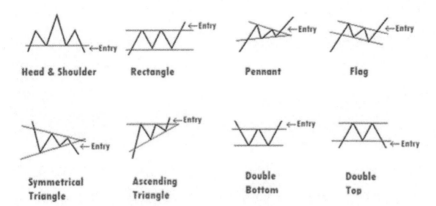

Image 1: A visual representation of all price patterns that indicate entry and exit points in the financial markets.

How to Set Up A Stop Loss

When setting up a trade, you will always be given the option to pick a price point at which you automatically sell to protect yourself from any more loss should the price fall lower. A different kind of stop-loss is an order that a trader gives to sell their position in an asset when it falls below a certain point after initially rising. You give the order to sell even if the asset has not reached the price you anticipated simply because it would be more damaging to wait it out, especially if the price wobbles. When set during the buying process, a stop-loss order automatically activates a sell order when the threshold is reached.

After setting the first stop-loss order, it is customary for a trader to adjust the stop-loss order upward after their asset rises in price. This protects the profits earned so far but keeps you in the game so that you don't miss out on further rises in price. This type of stop-loss adjustment is called a trailing stop. It comes in handy in very volatile markets and is the reason why hot markets are viable trading opportunities in the early stages when prices are rising consistently. With a trailing stop-loss order, you can activate a sell order at any time and avoid the losses associated with the free-fall prices of the blow-off phase.

Determining how to set up a stop loss is all about understanding yourself and the amount of risk you can put up with. After determining your risk tolerance, there are three techniques you can use to set your stop loss level; percentage, moving average, and support. With the percentage method, you simply determine the percentage of your position you are willing to lose. If you buy an asset at $100 and your risk tolerance is 10%, then you can set a stop loss at $90. The moving average method is a little bit more complicated to implement. With it, you first have to establish an asset's moving average over the long term. Prices tend to fall just above or below the moving average. So if the moving average for your current asset that is priced at $47 is $45, then you can set your stop loss at around $42.5. Finally, we have the support method of setting a stop loss level. Here, you put your stop-loss level just below the most recent support price of the asset you are buying. A lot more technical analysis goes into the support method of setting a stop loss, but it is a lot more effective because it follows the current price pattern of an asset.

Profit Taking Strategies

If you are hoping to make money swing trading, then you are definitely going to need a sound profit strategy. Your profit strategy determines the kind of stocks you target for trading and also the prices at which you enter and exit your trades. In profit taking, the exit point is the most important aspect. It determines whether you exit profitably or lose money. Unless you identify a really bullish asset, the exit point should rest at about 20% above the entry point.

The first strategy is called the hard and fixed exit. With this one, a trader identifies the most suitable point to exit a position and indicates it clearly on their chart. With this one, you position an exit at that point and no other (except perhaps the stop-loss level). The hard and fixed exit is suitable for automated traders who may not have the time to hit the sell button to sell when it comes down to it. The main disadvantage of this strategy is that you might sell at your fixed point and watch as the price rises far beyond, missing out on greater profits.

Second, we have the soft and variable exit, which is basically the opposite of the hard and fixed type. It requires the trader to keep an eye on the asset and exit at the most profitable level possible. This strategy is rather time-consuming because you will have to keep your eye on the live price charts to determine the best exit point.

The third exit strategy is the hard and variable kind in which the trader takes a kind of middle ground between the two strategies stated above. It is essentially a best-of-both-worlds situation, with the trader setting a fixed exit point but retaining the right to move it at any point. When it is automated, the hard and variable profit taking strategy uses trailing stop loss orders.

Finally, the fourth strategy of taking profits entails taking them partially. It gives you the chance to exit a position partially, leaving the rest of your money to appreciate while you cover your bases. Partial profit taking also reduces the potential losses you could suffer should the market reverse midway through the trade.

Selling Into Strength Vs. Selling Into Resistance

Can you time the financial market? It is a question that elicits very mixed reactions from analysts, divides them right along the middle as it were. Conservative market analysts denounce the practice while the more aggressive analysts advocate for market timing. For traders who time the market, they hold off on giving the sell order until the asset reaches its highest price possible (selling into resistance). Conservative traders prefer to take their profits while the market is still going strong, choosing assured profits now over the promise of greater profits in the future (selling into strength).

Selling into strength is the practice of taking profits that focuses on the current price rather than future forecast and the trend. It is encouraged to sell into strength if your trade reaches 25-30% above the entry point because at this point a lot of new orders often cause the asset to pull back and reverse downward.

With selling into resistance, profit maximization is the name of the game. A trader rides the curve right until it starts dropping rather than pulling out prematurely. Selling at resistance has another advantage. When the price reverses downward, you can flip from a long to a short position, maximizing your profits substantially because you make money going up and going down. However, you should take care not to get caught in the sideways pull of the markets.

Chapter 10: 2 Insanely Profitable Trading Setups

A trading setup is the formation of a tradable price chart that is typically indicated by a pattern or other indicator (gap, reversal, etc.). Knowing the point at which to start trading is extremely important. As you develop your swing trading strategy, you should come up with a few trading setups that you can use, almost automatically, to identify potentially profitable trading opportunities. In this chapter, we shall look at two trading setups in particular, namely price spike and "copy the big boys", and tell you how you can set them up in Finviz.

Setup 1: Price Spike Strategy

The price of assets often spikes upward without warning, sometimes defying logical technical analysis or rising higher than you would expect. When price spikes happen, they may remain high for a few minutes or a few hours, giving traders a very slim window of opportunity to trade. But a spike in price is useless if you learn about it after it has already started. In fact, joining the bandwagon and buying into a spiked or spiking asset is the mark of a novice trader. To establish yourself as a professional trader, you will have to identify the spikes before they actually happen. That way, you can take up a position before the price climbs and then sell when it actually goes up.

To identify a stock that is likely to spike, you can follow the fundamental route or use technical analysis tools. In fundamental analysis, an impending very positive and confidence-inspiring news article is a proven winner. With technical analysis, you will have to look at the 1-year return, the 10-day return, the average volumes, the exchange, asset price, and price versus 50-day average metrics.

Fortunately, you can get all these metrics of an asset using Finviz and I am going to tell you how.

The 1-Year Return

Assets that have been performing well in the past year are great investment opportunities. A stock, ETF, Forex, cryptocurrency, or option that has been trending upward consistently indicates massive confidence in the asset, which means that the chances of the asset spiking in price are very high. On average, you should look for assets that have appreciated over 40%. This way, even if your anticipated price hike does not happen, you can be assured of a little growth in price in the short time you will hold the asset. On Finviz, you can search the assets by their annual rate of return simply by inserting the metrics on the platform's search engine.

The 10-Day Return

After identifying the assets that have been growing strongly over the past year, it is time to go short term. Recent growth in stock price means that confidence has surged in the recent past. It could be caused by some anticipation among investors for some good news like great financial results, a new CEO, a merger, or just any sort of fundamental factor. On the other hand, it could just be caused by the recognition of the admirable run an asset has been having. As more traders and investors recognize the potential of an asset, the price goes up due to rising demand.

An 8% growth rate in the past week and a half shows a bullish asset that will continue to attract attention until the price peaks and then probably reverses due to oversubscription. The 10-day period catches all the assets that may not have been performing so great but that have consolidated previously. Again, you can simply insert the metrics and let Finviz do all the heavy lifting for you. And because the 10-day rate of return is a more short-term setup, it is a more accurate predictor of price spikes. When an asset has been trending low for some time, a period of gradual growth in price almost always precedes a spike.

Average Volume

The average volume of an asset denotes the amount traded over a given period of time and is calculated by dividing the total volume by the length of trading recorded. So from this, we get the average daily trading volume, the average weekly trading volume, and the average monthly trading volume. You can go as far as the quarter, the year, even past ten years, but these longer-time averages are rather unnecessary when identifying an asset to swing. The daily and weekly averages work best in this case. For the big market cap companies that receive massive investor interest, an average volume of over 100,000 is recommended. Companies with a lower market cap or those that have not been in the market for a long time but are exploding can be given a lower threshold. When trading internationally, like in Canada, a lower threshold of 10,000 is appropriate because the stock markets are smaller and they see a lot less trading. The average volume enables you to determine that an asset is not performing a certain way because of a few sizeable transactions. A large average also means that you will get buyers for your asset when it finally comes time to exit the position.

Price

The price of an asset determines the margins you can get from it when you sell. An asset going for $4.7 will give less profit at 20% than an asset that goes for $47 at the same profit margin. And because prices are indicated on a price chart by percentage, the lowest price of any asset you should consider for swing trading should be at least $5. This also makes it easier for you to avoid trash stocks. Good stocks ultimately break through the $5 price point.

Current Price Vs. The 50-Day Average

The prevailing price of an asset plays a big part in determining current and future prices. This is partly because traders everywhere study technical charts and because prices have a tendency to maintain their current trend until a reversal occurs. When identifying the best assets to trade in, you should compare the current price with the 50-day average and ensure that the current is at least 15% above the 50-day average. An asset whose current price compares in that manner with the 50-day average is likely to spike in the near future. And the higher the margin between the two prices, the higher the spike is likely to be. On Finviz, you can determine an asset's current price to the 50-day average ratio by entering your desired margin in the "above 50-day average" filters.

Stock Exchange

Finally, after identifying all these technical aspects of an asset, you have to decide what stock exchange you are going to attempt to swing it at. The same assets could sell at different prices in different stock exchanges, so deciding what stock exchange to buy your

Online Trading Masterclass

asset from should be an important part of the trade. Using Finviz, Chartmill, and other scanners, you can easily identify the best stock exchange to make your swing trade based on the prevailing price and other aspects like charges and taxation. The options open to you include the NYSE, NYSE Arca (Archipelago), Nasdaq, the Toronto Stock Exchange, Venture, and Over the Counter (OTC) trading.

Setup 2: The "Copy the Big Boys" Strategy

Coming up with a swing trading strategy can be quite challenging for the average trader. You have to learn a whole lot of strategies and technical analysis techniques and then probably be disappointed when a sudden and unexpected reversal or a complete misinterpretation of the market results in a loss for you. On the other end of the asset trading spectrum, we have the institutional traders. They include hedge funds, investment banks, and large brokerage firms. These big institutions hire up to thousands of analysts to crunch numbers and try to figure out the impending price changes of the stock markets and the assets traded therein. Large corporations buy small companies aggressively because they are growing and will one day be big companies with big price tags on their stock. Big players focus on the longer short-term duration of swing trading, looking for momentum and trends in smaller companies that have growing sales. Momentum is a principle that can be very profitable for the short-term swing trader as well. To determine momentum, we analyze the following metrics.

2-Year Return

Smaller market capitalization companies are often on the small side because they have been growing for a shorter period of time. For companies that have been trading publicly for a short time, the 2-year return indicates the growth pattern observed previously. For this category, we look at a 2-year return of 65% to determine stocks that present a good swing trading opportunity. The 2-year trend of other assets can similarly indicate trading potential.

Average Volume

The big boys target assets that have been averaging high volume trades. But unlike the 100,000-threshold discussed above, for momentum stocks, a smaller figure is used to account for the fact that smaller companies tend to have fewer volume trades overall.

Market Capitalization

When choosing the market capitalization for momentum stocks, we choose companies that have about $400 million in market cap. These stocks tend to move in larger percentage points than large-cap stocks because they are still in their aggressive growth stage. The relative anonymity of smaller companies gives them some mystery, making some of the more conservative investors stay away. But when the double digits growth results are announced, everyone takes notice and the price responds accordingly.

Price Vs 200-Day Average

Because momentum stocks are more of an unknown quantity, we need to look further than the 50 days discussed above. A 200-day average is therefore compared to the current price to determine those stocks that have been trending upward. But in this case, we use a 90% ratio so that we don't miss out on great trading opportunities because a stock happened to be going at a price a few cents or dollars below the 200-day average.

Sales Quarter-Over-Quarter Change

The sales results of a company have a huge impact on how investors view its future prospects. Massive growth in sales indicates a company that is establishing itself in its field as a strong competitor, possibly a future giant. A 20% growth in the sales figures from the current quarter to the same quarter the previous year indicates great potential for momentum trading.

Sales 1-Year Change

Apart from the quarter-to-quarter changes in price, the annual changes of a company's sales figures come in handy when looking at suitable stocks to swing. Again, we use the 20% level. However, we can raise the percentage to hone in on stocks that have a stronger growth pattern.

The Right Stock Exchange

The last thing you do when selecting a momentum stock, in accordance with the big boys, is to check the stock exchanges that are hot for the type of asset you intend to swing. For example, NASDAQ is the exchange of choice for tech companies. Your scanner will allow you to filter the different stock exchanges by the most suitable assets to trade there and filter every asset by the exchange best suited for its trading.

So there you have it, two of the most insanely profitable swing trading setups for you to try out. Even as you develop your own trading strategies, these two are tried, tested, and trusted methods. They have been used by institutional and retail traders alike to make huge profits, so their results are reliable enough. And even better, you can tweak and combine them easily, changing some of the filters to come up with an even better setup.

Chapter 11: Money Management

Picking the right setup is one side of the coin in swing trading. The other side is the art of money management. In this chapter, we shall look at the second part, which is perhaps more important for a trader looking to establish themselves as a profitable short-term investor in the financial markets. Money management is actually more important than the fundamental/technical analysis part because if you can't manage risk even as the best technical trader in the world, you will lose all your capital.

A lot of traders start their career with the rosy dreams of making it big in the financial markets with the one big trade. Trades like George Soros' shorting of the British pound to make $1 billion in just one day. This kind of thinking is very dangerous because it often results in the trader suffering one huge loss that knocks them off the game forever. Just like great profits are invigorating and inspirational, huge losses are demoralizing and discouraging. It takes discipline and patience and years of hard work to even get to the position that George Soros was during the British currency crisis of 1992.

The first and most important part of money management is the assessment of risk and reward. After determining the amount of risk you are willing to shoulder and the reward you are targeting with each trade, you should then manage the trade size to ensure that it is within the two metrics. Finally, every good trader keeps a trading journal as a record of the successful and unsuccessful trades they have made. This record then forms part of their trading strategy later on in their career. In the sections below, we discuss these principles of money management further.

Reward/Risk Assessment

Reward assessment is the task of determining the possible future events that could possibly bring a positive effect on a listed asset. A trader then determines the best way they can position themselves to benefit from the opportunity.

On the other hand, risk assessment is the process of identifying the events that are likely to happen in the future to bring about a negative impact on businesses and assets listed in the stock exchange. After identifying these factors, a trader then weighs up their tolerance for the risk brought about by these potential future events. Risk assessment is a three-step process.

First, we identify the exact event that is threatening to our asset. The exact event is referred to as a hazard, and the only way to be good at identifying risks is to expand your knowledge base. Hazards can either be internal or external. Internal risks are those brought about by internal factors while external factors are brought about by changes in the market structure. These include political turmoil, rising interest rates, natural disasters, and terrorist attacks.

The second step in identifying risk-causing hazards is the determination of how likely it is for an event to affect the markets. In risk assessment, we also determine the probable magnitude of this impact. The third step involves setting up the control measures needed to secure capital from losses in case the risk manifests.

Managing Trade Size

The second step in managing your money is determining how much of your capital you are going to commit on a given trade. Based on the risk and reward assessment, you determine how much you stand to lose, calculate it against how much you are likely to gain and find your risk/reward ratio. A risk/reward ratio of 2:1 is preferred by most investors because it allows them to double their money. But the trades that carry that kind of risk/reward ratio are few and far between. In most cases, trading opportunities carry a ratio between 11:10 (10% profit) and 5:4 (25% chance of profit).

The risk/reward ratio is important for the trader to determine the amount of money they are going to risk on a trade. Depending on how much capital you have in your trading portfolio, you can risk between 2% and 10%. For those traders with really small capital to trade with, a higher percentage of your capital in trade size is necessary to make a profit. But with a large portfolio running into the hundreds of thousands of dollars, lesser market positions should be taken. As a rule of thumb, 2% is the recommended level. And even though you can play around and increase your per-trade capital commitment, you should be careful to avoid over-committing, especially in those sure thing trades. They have a tendency to surprise you with losses where you expected a windfall.

Keeping A Trade Journal

A trading journal keeps a record of all the trading activities you did that ended in an exit whether profitable or not. The journal is your most honest self-reflection device. By going through it and revisiting your trading procedure, you can analyze your trading methods in an objective manner. This honest self-assessment is great for learning from your mistakes. It also helps you identify successful trades and how you executed them to give you a chance to do it again. A trade journal is also an important tool in the formulation of a trading strategy. The notes you insert between the pages will ultimately define your stock trading style.

A trading journal can be put into different media now. You have the good old writing pad, smartphone, tablet, and desktop computer. By journaling, you can indicate the prices of various assets on your charts and write down a list of market conditions in the prevailing weather at a particular time.

You can read this and be encouraged to conduct risk and reward analysis, set your trade size, and keep a trade journal but at the end of the day, there is nothing you can do to completely avoid losses. This poignant statement is actually the fifth **golden rule** of swing trading; success in swing trading is only attained by those traders who are able to maintain their cool after a loss and bounce right back into the game.

Chapter 12: Trading Lifestyle & Discipline

There is more to swing trading than staring at charts all day. Swing trading is one of those professions that require total commitment, which includes adopting the right lifestyle for it. Another thing about starting a swing trading gig is that you will be working for yourself. There will be no boss to yell at you and threaten to fire you if you don't do a good enough job. Instead, there will be your bills reminding you that if you don't do it right, you will probably go hungry and get kicked out of your house - no pressure. This is especially true for those full-time traders who will rely entirely on swing trading to put food on the table. For working people, the trick will be learning how to balance between your regular 9 to 5 with the swing trading side job.

That is why I have compiled a checklist of all the things you need to do to become a better trader. Even though some of the issues discussed in this section may come out as rather corny, each one of them plays a big role in getting you in the right frame of mind to start trading.

Eating Right

Your eating habits determine your decision-making capabilities. Studies have indicated time and time again that nutrition is very important in determining the mental capabilities a person exhibits. Because 30% of all the food you eat goes toward powering your brain, it is important that you ensure that what you put into your body is only the best and most nutritional food. Food type is another factor that determines our decision-making capabilities. The types of food you eat say much about you. The person who eats burgers and fries every day will have a very different demeanor and outlook for life compared to someone who eats more healthy and balanced foods.

Ensure that you get a balanced diet every day and be sure to only eat foods that are clean and organic. Showing greater responsibility about what you put in your body will keep your mind in a better state for when you start trading.

Finally, alcohol is a no-no during your trading hours. The last thing you want to do is make a bunch of ill-informed trades in a drunken haze. Alcohol compromises your mental faculties and impairs your judgment. An asset with a horrible set of technicals that you would never have considered sober suddenly looks very attractive when alcohol comes into play. I am not saying that you shouldn't crack open a bottle and toast to your good fortune after a particularly profitable trade, but staying away from the booze cabinet during trading hours is definitely something you should do.

Sleeping

There is a stereotypical belief that traders have to stay up all day and all night, trading in every stock exchange there is and catch every bit of news about the stock market. Here is the thing about this theory though; it is bonkers. You can be a successful swing trader, trade in all major stock exchanges and still have a full life. And you don't need to work 20 hours to do it! All you need to do is put together a nice suite of tools to get you on your way to profitability. In fact, by using the stock scanners and screeners discussed in chapter 2, you can reduce your workload substantially enough that you give yourself lots of free time to engage in whatever pastime you would like to occupy yourself with.

Studies show that 90% of people require between 6.5 to 8 hours of sleep at night to be fully rested. With the right tools and a simplified work process, you will have enough time to sleep up to 8 hours. Apart from the amount of sleep you get, you should make sure that you establish a regular sleep pattern. All news and alerts from Finviz, Scoop Markets, or any other scanner should be cut off at least 30 minutes before bed to allow your mind time to decompress. Before the actual falling asleep, you should also consider starting some bedtime activity, like meditation to keep your spiritual and mental balance up to par. Another bedtime rule you should observe is to not trade in bed. If you need to look at anything on your phone or laptop while in bed, then use the blue light filters to minimize the light glare to your eyes.

In the event of sleeplessness, be careful the sleeping aids you use. Magnesium sprays and drugs like Xanax are simply provisional solutions to a deeper problem. If you are having sleep issues, then you should definitely start meditating. It is a more wholesome and fulfilling solution.

Visualization

Visualization exercises are very helpful in helping you achieve your goals. Successful people use visualization to motivate themselves all the time. By visualizing the thing you desire, you get the willpower to fight through any setback until you attain it. A good way to start is to write down your goals, read it before starting your meditation session, and visualize yourself making successful trades. It may sound like some Zen Buddhist voodoo, but it works. As you visualize yourself making successful trades in the mind, your brain develops the skills you need to identify successful ones in real life. Visualization always results in more successful trades, not because the markets mysteriously align themselves to your will, but because your brain learns to recognize perfect winning price patterns.

Meditation

I have touched on it above, but it bears repeating. Meditation is not just the stuff for hippies or Buddhists. I learned about the effectiveness of meditation from a successful penny stock trader. You see, I was intrigued about this man who could make 6 figure profits every year from an asset that, by all indications, shouldn't be making anyone rich. But what he told me changed my perspective about spirituality forever. You wouldn't think that trading has anything to do with spirituality, but the necessity for being logical and unemotional when trading makes it quite a spiritual affair. And to be able to take emotions out of the equation when trading, you will have to get in touch with your emotions in ways that you haven't done before. You are going to have to start meditating.

Avoiding Burnout

Every activity that requires mental and physical energy to get it done has the power to exhaust your emotional energies. In the short term, working without breaking for some relaxation can be very detrimental. It is important that you take breaks from time to time. Stretch, drink some coffee, breath in some fresh air, and take a moment to free up your mind from the rigors of trading. In the long term, you will need to give yourself a non-working vacation every six months. A week's traveling or resting vacation where you simply kick back and regroup will do you a lot of good. This brings us to our sixth golden rule; in the long term, your wealth moves in direct proportion to your health. Take care of your health and you will empower yourself to create riches beyond your wildest imagination.

Chapter 13: Trading Taxation for Dummies

Let me start by saying that this will arguably be the least sexy chapter of this book. I may also add that it is the most important because the last thing you want is to find yourself facing an IRS investigation. To understand the basic concepts of taxation for swing trading, you need to understand cost basis, capital gains, and capital losses. Cost basis is calculated by adding up the original price of an asset by commission and other charges. Capital gains are basically the margin between what you sell an asset at and the price at which you bought it. Capital losses happen when at the end of a trade you end up with less money than you started off with.

Classification

The distinction in taxation in the financial markets is between long term and short-term investors. The trader falls under the category of the short-term investor and all trades must be held for less than one year to qualify as short term investment. Other defining features of traders include spending much of your time buying and selling assets. A regular buying pattern is also required for one to be defined by the tax code as a trader. The final quality is that one must aim to profit from short-term fluctuations in price rather than the long term. This is the more definitive feature, and more importantly, it is the one the government uses to set the taxation rates for traders and investors.

The swing trader somehow gets lost in the definitions between traders and investors. But because the main defining feature of the tax code is the duration of trades, your one day to a few months' trades will have to be classified as trades. Swing traders are thus taxed using the traders' tax code.

Tax Rates

Assets in the lower tax brackets held for less than a year attract a capital gains tax of 15% at the lowest level while investment in the 10-15% tax bracket remains at 0%. And when the highest earning investor pays 25% of their capital gains in tax, the highest tax bracket with trading attracts an exorbitant 39.6% tax. Basically, trading is viewed as a normal income-generating activity. This is perhaps because it has been designed to cater for day traders, who are actually professional traders who buy and sell assets on a full-time basis.

Benefits

The tax rate of short-term trades is almost twice as high as that of long term trades. But the trader also gets some benefits, including a deduction on net capital loss of up to $3,000. Another benefit is a clause that allows you to write off any money above 2% of your gross income so that you are able to deduct your personal exemptions and take full advantage of tax breaks for higher income tax categories. Schedule C filing also negates the need to pay self-employment tax.

A wash sale tax exemption is another distinct advantage enjoyed by traders. The rule is, any asset you sell at a loss gets written off and does not factor into the calculation of your tax obligation. This rule inspired an IRS measure that stipulates that if you, your spouse, or a business you control buys an asset you wrote off as a loss within 30 days of you selling it, the original loss is disallowed. To jump this hurdle, you become a mark-to-market trader. To do this, you will have to pretend to sell all your asset holdings, taking in your imaginary gains and losses. When you start the next trading year with your old assets, it appears as though you re-purchased all your assets. Being a mark-to-market trader also grants you the right to deduct an infinite amount of losses, not just the $3,000 allowed to traders in general.

Preparation

April is a hard month for beginner traders. You embark upon the journey of filing your tax returns and realize that the IRS is not interested in just the profits and losses you made on your sales. A detailed description is also needed. Trying to remember hundreds of trades in a few weeks can be a very daunting exercise, especially when done under pressure. To save yourself the trouble, you should start off right. You should keep a record of the asset you trade, the price you bought it for and the sale price, the date of purchase and selling, and the position size you took up. With all these details meticulously recorded for every trade, you will sail smoothly during the filing season, a time that is otherwise nightmarish for most traders. Understand the tax implications of swing trading before you begin. It is important that you read widely on the topic and where necessary, consult a tax attorney for more clarification. The less the amount of time you spend tussling with the IRS, the more the trading time you will leave yourself, and thus the more the profits you will make.

Conclusion

In conclusion, we are going to refresh on the 7 golden rules stated throughout this book. I believe that by following these 7 guidelines to swing trading, you can establish yourself as a very successful one and finally manage to live the kind of lifestyle you have always desired.

First and foremost, your trading career should fit around your current or preferred lifestyle. You should never let your trading dictate how you live your life.

Second, exercise great caution whenever you encounter "hot markets." If it looks too good to be true, then it probably is. But even with the high risk of loss, hot markets or bubbles can be quite profitable if you approach them with the greatest caution and set trailing stops on all your trades. That way, you protect the profits earned at any point and may sell automatically when the prices start failing.

The greatest commandment when it comes to actually entering and exiting the market is that you only buy after a wave of selling has occurred and sell after a wave of buying has occurred. Barring the occurrence of an external stimulus that prompts you to buy or sell outside of these parameters, you should always observe this principle. This practice of moving against the market allows you to take advantage of low prices to buy and high prices to sell.

The third golden rule of swing trading is that when doing your market research, social media should be a resource but not the entire market research strategy. It should come as a supplement to other tools like scanners and screeners and make up part of a suite of tools that greatly boost your trading capabilities.

The fourth rule of swing trading is that you should never risk more than 10% of your capital in any one trade. You may adjust this figure upward or downward depending on the amount of capital you have to start with, going as low as 2% if you have at least $100,000 in capital.

Successful traders are not those who never make losses. They are the ones who are disciplined enough to bounce back from losses. It may take a few months and a whole lot of losses to get the hang of it but once you do, you will start making more profitable trades more frequently.

The sixth golden rule states that taking care of your health is very important. The demanding nature of swing trading should not come between you and a healthy lifestyle. In fact, you will find that your wealth will grow in direct proportion with your health. So to build your wealth, start by building your health.

Finally, and this is very important, you've got to understand the tax code and how it affects you as a swing trader. Compliance with the tax code starts with understanding the tax code which is too complex to exhaust in this short excerpt. But here's a clue you might find useful; keep an accurate record of all trades.

You don't need to win every trade you enter. That is a distinction even the best traders in the world don't meet. Instead, you can target a 55% success rate, which will make you enough money to cover the losses of the other 45% of your trades. As long as you manage your money right, the stock markets are going to be a very profitable venture for you.

And as you start your swing trading career, just remember that it is a profession that takes a while to really master. You will have to be patient and try as much as possible to enjoy the journey. The small wins may not seem very huge at first, but they are very important. If you learn to enjoy them even as you pursue greater rewards, you will find that your career in swing trading will be more successful than it would be if you were to spend it chasing the big win.

Glossary

These are the terms that you will hear about in the stock market. Understand them for a more profitable trading experience.

Arbitrage: the buying and selling of an asset in different stock markets.

Averaging down: the practice of buying an asset while the price is dropping

Bear market: a market that is experiencing an overall downward movement in the price of listed assets.

Blue chip stocks: the stocks of large companies with a huge lead over their competitors.

Bull market: a market that is experiencing a resurgence in the prices of listed assets.

Brokers: the people who, for a fee, connect buyers with sellers in the stock market and vice versa.

Bid: the price at which a trader is willing to buy an asset

Close: the time of day when all activity in the stock market comes to an end

Execution: the completion of a buy or sell order

Index: a benchmark used to measure the performance of different sectors of the stock market

Leverage: the buying of shares or any other asset from a broker on credit

Order: the bid a trader makes to buy a certain amount of assets

Quote: the value of an assets latest trading activity

Rally: a rapid rise in the price of an asset

Sector: a group of stocks, assets, or commodities in the same industry

Short selling: the practice of borrowing shares from someone at high prices with the promise to return them later when the price goes down.